Reimagining God

Reimagining God

By faith Abraham obeyed God when he was called to go out . . . and he went out, not knowing where he was to go.

—**Hebrews 11:8**

Whatever your heart clings to and confides in, that is really your god.

—**Martin Luther**

People once knew, or thought they knew, what they meant when they spoke of God, and they spoke of him often. Now in the course of a day's business we may not mention him at all. The name of God seems to have been retired from everyday discourse.

—*In Search of Deity,* John Macquarrie, Gifford Lectures, 1983

We must move beyond a spirituality focused on the divine and the human, to a spirituality concerned with the survival of the natural world in its full splendour, fertility and integral well-being.

—**Thomas Berry,** Catholic priest, 1914–2009

Reimagining
GOD

The Faith Journey of a Modern Heretic

Foreword by Tom Hall

Lloyd Geering

POLEBRIDGE PRESS
Salem, Oregon

Cover and interior design by Robaire Ream

Library of Congress Cataloging-in-Publication Data
Geering, Lloyd, 1918-
[Essays. Selections]
Reimagining God : the faith journey of a modern heretic / by Lloyd Geering; with a foreword by Tom Hall.
      pages cm
Includes bibliographical references and index.
ISBN 978-1-59815-156-5 (alk. paper)
1. God. I. Title.
BL473.G36 2014
231--dc23

                                                    2014025148

Contents

Foreword

It was quite a journey that young Lloyd Geering set out upon seventy-nine years ago. Surely none of those he knew in 1935 could have imagined that this seventeen-year-old—a New Zealand farm boy who by his own account was "somewhat bashful" and "very immature", who daily rode the train to Dunedin to attend Otago Boys' High School and home again to care for the animals and cut wood—might one day be Sir Lloyd Geering, the recipient of his country's highest honour. And except for the well-documented facts, one would have equal difficulty in believing that this brilliant but unchurched freshman who entered the University of Otago in 1936 was beginning a trek that would lead to his election as head of New Zealand's Presbyterian theological seminary, to popular acclaim as a columnist and lecturer on a wide range of subjects, and to worldwide recognition as a theologian and scholar of comparative religion. And as the remote parish of Kurow got to know their newly ordained pastor in 1943, they could have had no inkling that twenty-four years hence both his position as Principal of Knox College and his ordination would be threatened by charges brought against him in the church's National Assembly. For in 1967 he dared to follow the lead of the best theological scholars of the day in proposing what was widely accepted by theologians but carefully kept from the people in the pews: that Jesus' resurrection was the stuff of ecstatic experiences rather than an historical event.

What enabled that unobtrusive teenager to take on the challenges of university life with such éclat that he earned first class
honours in pure mathematics? What led him to sense a call to the
ministry? Why was it that wherever his career led, he was soon
chosen to be what we incurably colloquial Americans call 'the
go-to guy'—committee chairman, assembly delegate, spokes-
man, conference organizer, Principal, and at last Founding Chair
of a university department? In short, what were the ingredients
of his steady rise to prominence?

Let me suggest four primary qualities. First, he possessed an
imposing intellect equally adept at both analytic and synthetic
modes of thought. From this came an unflinching honesty, for
the deductive mathematician was always yoke-fellow to the in-
ductive empiricist. Second, an ingrained sensitivity that no doubt
stemmed from a sometimes unsettled and solitary youth led early
in high school to active membership in the Student Christian
Movement, a genuine concern for others, and a determination
to lead a useful life. And from honesty and resolve arose a third
dynamic—a greater esteem for actions than for beliefs, for deeds
than words, and the resulting work ethic that produced both
an astonishing catalogue of activities and a lifelong regimen of
voluminous reading. Last, and I suspect at least equally important, was an endless curiosity, a passion to understand the ever-
changing and constantly evolving world we live in and to make
it known to others. Like Chaucer's Clerk, 'gladly wolde he lerne,
and gladly teche'.

Geering's fascinating autobiography provides ample testament
that his intellectual and spiritual enlightenment did not begin
with a flash of insight or a sudden conversion experience, but
that it represents the accumulation of a lifetime of study and
service dedicated to the complementary tasks of making sense of
the human condition and realizing his own full potential. And
in a world habitually devoted to the status quo, that necessarily
meant causing a fair amount of friction. John Shelby Spong re-

cently summed it up nicely: "For the past fifty years he has been
a voice calling organized religion to deal with reality."

Yet despite his involvement in several major controversies
and notwithstanding some of the highly unorthodox assertions
that may be found in this brief survey of his thinking, one must
not suppose that he has always been preoccupied with challenging traditional Christianity. To be sure, while yet a seminarian
he became aware of the general scholarly agreement that most
of the long-revered narratives of the Hebrew Bible were more
legendary than historical (though broaching that subject might
endanger a minister's hope for continued employment). Still,
although his New Testament professors had begun the job of
disabusing the fledgling preacher of the dubious notion that the
gospels constitute a more or less accurate record of events, as
late as 1955 Geering took Luke's story of the encounter on the
road to Emmaus to be essentially historical. Soon after, however,
he began reading Bultmann and Tillich, and came to recognize
that Christian faith was tied to an outmoded worldview, and
knew that doctrines based on a dualistic view of the universe
could no longer be honestly defended. Thus as late as 1999 he
doubted the possibility of obtaining any appreciable amount of
reliable knowledge about the words and deeds of Jesus. That
opinion, too, would at last yield to evolutionary forces: by 2001
the work of Bob Funk and the Jesus Seminar had so altered his
outlook that in 2010 he published a series of lectures entitled
Jesus Rediscovered.

In short, Geering's understanding of religion has from the
beginning been a work in progress, an evolving body of thought
that has embraced many fields of knowledge and as a result become ever more inclusive. In Chapters 3–12 of this book that
diversity and inclusivity will be evident, together with the corollary necessity of being ready to adopt new insights and question
old boundaries. For since our understanding of the world we
live in is constantly evolving, no religious belief or doctrine can

be considered absolute or final. The collective faith journey of humankind must be as amenable to course corrections as that of the individual pilgrim—especially in the increasingly secular culture of the twenty-first century. For it becomes ever clearer that in today's brave new world one important criterion of religious truth must be its congruence with the observable facts of the universe. And this growing recognition is what makes progressive theologians like Don Cupitt, Gordon Kaufman, and Lloyd Geering so attractive to those who seek a new frame of reference for their pursuit of authentic human existence.

Taken together, then, these lectures do considerably more than trace the intellectual and spiritual journey of one erudite scholar, for he has always aimed his thoughts at 'people like myself, people who were seeking to make some sense of this awe-inspiring yet bewildering universe, and to find some purpose in their lives'. Indeed, I would suggest that his compilation presents a portrait of a contemporary prophet who, in the manner of the prophets of old, not only tells us how we have created our present spiritual ambiguities and ecological muddles, but also indicates what steps we must take to avoid planetary disaster. And he links the two by offering a new meaning for an ancient symbol, by reminding us what we have long known but too easily forget: that 'God' is not the name of a being, but a symbol by which we express our highest ideals, our fundamental values, our deepest yearnings, and our ultimate concerns. In short, Geering urges us to see things as they are, and challenges us to make our increasingly global and secular world a sustainable one as well—something we can do, he believes, by undertaking a journey of faith that will attune our lives to the unseen Presence and Process that has long been referred to as God.

—**Tom Hall**

Preface

We spend much of our lives looking forward to events yet to come, often trying to peer into the future. In modern times this practice has developed into quite an industry, not only for novelists like H. G. Wells but even more for economists, social planners and the like. I plead guilty to this habit by having written *Tomorrow's God* and *The World to Come*.

Yet like the biblical Abraham who "went out not knowing where he was to go", we have no certain way of knowing what lies ahead of us and so of necessity we journey into the unchartered territory of the future somewhat blindly. Sometimes it is only by looking back that we are able to discern clearly the direction we have been taking. While the story of Lot's wife may warn us of the dangers of looking back, it is only by doing so that we are able to appreciate the nature of the journey we have travelled. In the journey of life, it is by looking back that we gain much insight into the kind of persons we have become and how much our thinking has changed as the years have gone by. No doubt we all engage in this exercise from time to time, but understandably much more so as we get older.

Ten years ago I was required to look back over my earlier life in a rather public way when invited to participate in a series of lectures on the theme of 'God and Me'. (That lecture now begins this collection.) Previously I had avoided speaking publicly about myself for fear of sounding egotistical and self-important. Yet not only was this lecture greeted with a more positive response than I expected, but I found the preparation of it to be a very re-warding exercise in self-understanding. So thereafter I set out to develop it into an autobiography, eventually published in 2008 as *Wrestling with God*. The title was drawn from the biblical tale of Jacob at the Wadi Jabbok; it is one that symbolically describes the destiny of the people of Israel. But, on looking back, I had found that it neatly summed up my own faith journey.

So it is not entirely accidental that this autobiographical ex-ercise should have led me to look back even further. I went on to spend more than two years in catching up on what cosmolo-gists, biologists, archaeologists and historians are now able to tell us about our human past and how we evolved within this awe-inspiring and ever-expanding universe. One might call this 'looking back on the grand scale' for we now learn that it all started over thirteen billion years ago. Our minds find it difficult to cope with the very magnitude of the universe both in space and in time. Yet even more mind-boggling than that is the way life has evolved on this planet—ever so slowly at first, during the two billion years of only micro-organisms, and accelerating in the last half billion years. Only in the last tiny segment of cosmic time did this evolving process bring forth the speaking apes we now call humans.

Such knowledge as we now have, amassed only in the last two hundred years, constitutes an awe-inspiring story that I at-tempted to sketch in *From the Big Bang to God*. The experience of understanding and absorbing this story can have a mind-changing effect on us. In particular, as the title indicates, the traditional way of understanding the relationship between the universe and God has become reversed. Far from delineating an original supernatural creator to explain the universe, we now find that the cosmos is itself self-creative. It consists wholly of energy that manifests an amazing creativity through its tendency to form itself into ever more complex entities. First came the atoms, then molecules joined to form cells, which finally combined into organisms. The human species is the most complex organism we know of in the universe, having emerged only very recently after a very lengthy process of evolution.

But we, being entirely one with the universe, have in turn manifested that same creativity by inventing language. By first inventing names and concepts we began to create our own subjective world, one that may be called a world of thought. It serves as the lens through which we see and understand the world we live in. We inherit it from our ancestors, add a little to it ourselves and pass it on to our descendants. In only a few thousand years this thought world has evolved, moving through the stories of the gods we call myths until it became the philosophies and sciences that engage the attention of educated people today.

In short, the universe is an evolving process that manifests continual creativity: it created us and we in turn created, for example, the idea of God. The concept of God as the creator of everything may be judged one of the most important ideas humans ever invented. Of course it was not created in a moment of time, as some modern concepts are, but it slowly evolved over time. God has a history! It became the foundation stone of the two great civilizations—Christian and Islamic—by providing them with an ultimate reference point for both knowledge ('Only God knows', as we commonly said) and power ('God is almighty'). This enabled our ancestors to see the world they lived in as a unity (a *uni*-verse), one that was permeated by a consistency that was open to reasoned enquiry. The idea of a Creator God motivated human minds to learn how his presumed creativity operated. They tried to understand what they called 'the ways of God' or what we now call 'the laws of nature'. Thus, even if by a somewhat tortuous route, the idea of God was instrumental in leading us to invent the empirical method used by modern science to increase our knowledge. The new knowledge has opened the way to the greatly advanced forms of technology and put into human hands new sources of power—steam, electricity, nuclear and electronic. We humans now increasingly share in what used to be regarded as the omniscience and omnipotence of God.

But we have reached a crucial point in our cultural evolution because the idea of God (after bequeathing to us so much) has now become problematical. That is why, by the middle of the twentieth century, theologians began to speak of the 'death of God'. More recently Richard Dawkins with his *God Is a Delusion* and Christopher Hitchens in his *God Is Not Great* have militantly rejected the idea of God as a dangerous falsehood. When taken simply as a comment on today's cultural situation, what they say contains much truth; but when we look at the role played by the idea of God over the millennia of evolving human culture, a rather different assessment emerges. In its time the *idea* of God *was* great in that it provided for us an ultimate point of reference that enabled us to reach the knowledge and power we now possess. Now, it appears, this God is slowly disappearing from the cultural scene, remaining only as a symbol that each of us must to interpret as we find best.

But where does this leave the human race, now bereft of an ultimate point of reference? This is a question I have been puzzling over during the last twenty years. So when Polebridge Press invited me to follow up the publication of *From the Big Bang to God* with a collection of my recent public lectures, it seemed to be an appropriate time to look back once more, though this time over quite a short span. Along what path has my faith journey been taking me over the last twenty years? To this end I have selected fourteen lectures and present them not chronologically, but in an order that shows the general direction in which I have been moving and why. It may be regarded as an appendix to *Wrestling with God*, but this time I have been wrestling with the increasing absence of God. It seemed appropriate to entitle the collection *Reimagining God*. Of course these lectures document only one person's path of faith but because we humans of all cultural and religious backgrounds are now facing the same global challenges, it is my hope that they may be of some help to others as they try to sort out their thoughts in this rapidly changing world.

PART 1

The Starting Point

God and Me

I have been invited to tell you what important lessons my life journey thus far has taught me about God. I cannot remember when I was first introduced to 'God'. My family did not regularly attend church, and though from the age of five to twelve my mother sent me to the nearest Presbyterian or Methodist Sunday School, I took this to be simply part of the normal growing-up process. Sunday School seemed much the same as daily school, where we also had weekly Religious Instruction, and so I felt no sense of holiness in it. I *was* aware of different kinds of churches, because a girl of my age from the Catholic family next door told me with pride that in her church God was kept locked up in a box on the altar. But already I had absorbed sufficient prejudice to dismiss this claim as just another of the Catholic superstitions that we Protestants condemned.

I do remember at the age of eleven discussing with one of my boyhood friends whether Christianity was really true. We came to the conclusion that it must be, or else people would not spend so much money building big churches. Thus I reached my teens with no strong convictions which either affirmed or denied Christian beliefs. An aunt presented me with a Bible that I started to read, but I began to lose interest when I reached the genealogies in Genesis. Nevertheless, I held my last Sunday

---

This public lecture was delivered in Pitt Street Uniting Church, Sydney, on October 22, 2004.

School in great esteem because it had the best children's lending library in the city, and I could take out new books every Sunday.

When I began high school my family moved back to New Zealand from Victoria, whereupon my Sunday School days were over and I had no further connection with the church for the next six years. In 1936 I started university and happened to find a room in a Roman Catholic home. The landlady had a son who was a priest, and her daughter belonged to the closed order of the Carmelites. I was much impressed by the devoutness of the home and was happy to join them in eating fish on Fridays.

All this made me begin to question my own position as a nominal, non-church-going Presbyterian, yet it did not prompt me to do anything about it. One Sunday near the end of that year, a fellow student who had been in my class all through high school invited me for the evening meal at his home. After the meal he told me the family would be going to church and asked whether I would like to join them. I would and I did, and I remember thinking during the service that it would not cause me any harm to begin attending church, and that I might learn something from the preaching.

So when I returned to university the following year I began to go to church, and at my friend's invitation joined him in the activities of the Student Christian Movement (SCM). I soon found myself attending a Bible class, going to church twice on Sunday, singing in the choir, and even teaching in Sunday School—in addition to becoming fully involved in the activities of the very strong SCM. In short, 1937 was the year when the direction and style of my life changed quite dramatically.

One could call it a conversion, but what had it all to do with God? It never occurred to me to say I had found God, or even that God had found me. Insofar as I thought of God at all, he was simply part of a total package. I was aware, of course, that I was consciously embracing the Christian tradition, and thus making a positive decision to walk the Christian way.

And why did I do so—and so willingly and enthusiastically? Because it so effectively filled a kind of spiritual vacuum in my life, a vacuum of which until that time I had lived unaware. The Christian story and everything associated with it provided me with a frame of reference that gave direction and meaning to my desire to make something of my life. Up until this time I had been drifting along, dutifully doing what my parents, teachers, and peers expected of me; suddenly I began to see life through new eyes. I was not aware of any special relationship with God, of the kind I heard some others tell, yet I did submit myself to a programme of daily devotional exercises, assuming that would perhaps lead me to have some experience of the reality of God. But the only form in which such an awareness came to me was a growing yet uncertain conviction that I was being called by God to study for the ministry.

Accordingly, at the beginning of 1938 I applied to the Presbyterian Church to be accepted as a theological candidate. I was secretly hoping I would be rejected as unsuitable because of my lack of church background, for this would have indicated that my conviction of being called by God was simply a psychological aberration. In fact, I felt no particular attraction to the life of parish ministry, about which I knew precious little in any case.

With its all too frequent lack of wisdom and insight, however, the church accepted me and greatly shaped my subsequent life. I was now living for some chosen purpose, and I delighted in that. Although it led in quite a different direction from what I might otherwise have chosen, I still tended to accept and believe what other Christians told me. I was advised to continue with my studies in Mathematics, and to enter the Theological College only after I had completed my Honours Degree.

Upon beginning my three-year theological course, I largely accepted everything I was taught. After all, my teachers were supposed to know all about the Christianity I had decided to embrace, and I was only a novice. Still, I was not wholly uncritical.

When I had enquired about joining the church in 1937, I recalled my initial introduction to the Bible and asked the minister, 'I'm not expected to believe all that stuff about Adam and Eve, am I?' 'Oh no', he said, 'No one in the church takes that story literally these days'. Some years later I was surprised to find that many people in the church still did just that.

But I was fortunate in being taught by theologians who were thoroughly immersed in what was known as Protestant liberalism. I was shown how to study the Bible using the modern methods of historical and literary criticism. To tell the truth, I found systematic theology boring even though my professor had written our highly regarded textbook, *The Organism of Christian Truth*. I was much more interested in church history, for it showed me how Christian faith and practice had evolved out of simple beginnings and thereafter gone through many changes. Years later this helped persuade me that instead of indoctrinating lay people with creeds and confessions presented as unchangeable truths, it would have been much more worthwhile to make them well informed about the story of Christianity and present it as a living and changing response to life.

But the most interesting part of my theological training was the study of the Bible, particularly in the original languages of Greek and Hebrew. This material seemed to provide a more solid base to the Christian tradition than abstract doctrines. I responded wholeheartedly to the proposition that the Christian message could be defended and expounded by appeal to historical testimony.

The liberal Protestantism in which I was being educated affirmed Christianity as the historical religion *par excellence*. Its foundation was not to be found chiefly in divinely revealed truths, but in historical events. The self-revelation of the Deity was more likely to be found by interpreting such narratives as the Exodus from Egypt, the Incarnation, or the Resurrection of Christ than in a dogmatic system or in the exact words of the Bible. Reliable testimony portrayed its central figure, Jesus Christ, as an historical figure; the Incarnation was an historical event; the God worshipped by Christians was the Lord of history.

But how did I relate to God in all of this? Looking back sixty years later, I realise that I was still uncritically accepting the being of God as part of the total Christian package. It certainly seemed to make some sense to say he was the Creator of the world—even if he was distant and beyond all human understanding. I understand now that I was more a deist than a theist: I was always rather suspicious of evangelicals who loved to ask, 'Do you believe in a personal God?' and who treated God as a friendly protector.

My third sermon, written while still a student, was entitled 'What is God like?' This suggests to me now that I was genuinely puzzled about the being of God and was keen to find an answer. Yet the academic statements about God that I studied in textbooks left me unenlightened. Thereafter I was happy to think of 'God' as the name of the ultimate mystery of life, and during the years of my ministry rarely preached about God. I felt I was on more solid ground in preaching about the way the Gospels portrayed Jesus Christ, but even then my grounding in the sciences made me steer clear of the so-called miracles. Believing it was my task to expound the Bible in order to provide insights on how best to live the Christian life, I found more than enough material in the Old and New Testaments.

Wishing to continue my studies during my ministry, I decided the best approach was to prepare for an Honours degree. My decision to concentrate on the Old Testament turned out to be a fortuitous one, for some years later it led me to embark on what became my main career. Although I found much in the parish ministry that was deeply satisfying, I had entered it not so much by choice as in response to a sense of duty. I discovered that I much preferred the role of teacher, for many aspects of the parish ministry proved frustrating. So it was that when one day I spotted an advertisement of the Presbyterian Church of Queensland inviting applications for a new Chair of Old Testament studies, I submitted my name. I felt no great sense of call this time; it was just something I would love to do—and it did not entail the repudiation of my original sense of call.

I held little hope of being successful, but successful I was, and this became another turning point in my life. I could now devote myself full time to study, and the best way of learning any subject is to teach it. Besides, Old Testament study was no longer very controversial: all the great battles about the supposed Mosaic authorship of the Pentateuch had been fought in the previous century. One was now free to study and explain the Old Testament as a collection of human documents that reflected the somewhat narrow beliefs and even prejudices of their authors.

Such was not yet the case with the New Testament, which even most liberal scholars accepted as a reasonably authentic record of the deeds and words of Jesus. The great exception to this traditional position was Rudolf Bultmann and his followers. Having already learned how to interpret the myths and legends in the book of Genesis, I was attracted to Bultmann's assertion that the New Testament message had for too long been imprisoned in the mythological world-view of the first century, and that to make it relevant to the modern world it needed to be 'demythologised'—that is, radically reinterpreted to reflect a twentieth-century understanding of reality. Despite my failure to realise it, my interests were already beginning to move beyond the limits of the Old Testament.

The widening of my theological interests was facilitated by the fact that I was invited by the University of Queensland to introduce a course on what was then called comparative religion—the study of religions other than Christianity. More by accident than by design I was already partially equipped for this task, for as early as my student days I had opted to sit a paper in comparative religion for the Melbourne post-graduate degree of

Bachelor of Divinity, even though no such course was offered at my college. Few theological colleges offered courses in the new discipline of comparative religion that had emerged only in the nineteenth century. The Catholic scholar, Ronald Knox, put his finger on the reason when he said, 'The study of comparative religion makes one comparatively religious'.

But it seemed to me that to fully appreciate the value of the Christian path of faith one should have some understanding of the alternative paths. Actually, there is a natural affinity between Old Testament Studies and Comparative Religion, because the Hebrew Bible explicitly contrasts monotheism with the religions of the ancient Semitic world out of which it emerged. I suspect that is why Wheeler Robinson and T. H. Robinson, two of the foremost Old Testament scholars of the early twentieth century, came to write books on comparative religion.

On my return to New Zealand in 1960 to take up the Chair of Old Testament in my alma mater, I was rather sorry to give up teaching comparative religion. Nevertheless I began to read a number of significant books that influenced my thinking on the subject of God. One was the three-volume *Systematic Theology* of Paul Tillich. Here at last I found a theologian who, like the biblical scholar Rudolf Bultmann, was aware he was living in the twentieth century. From him I learned that the idea of God was closely related to whatever concerned a person in an ultimate way. Second, I encountered Dietrich Bonhoeffer, who realised in a Nazi prison why it was no longer possible to be religious in the traditional way and who set forth a way of being Christian in the modern secular world.

Third, I was introduced to the Jesuit scientist Pierre Teilhard de Chardin, whose exciting magnum opus, *The Phenomenon of Man*, I read over one weekend almost without putting it down. Here was a vision of the cosmos that combined all we had come to know of physics, chemistry, biology, and theology into one ongoing story. I was awestruck. This visionary sketch of an evolving universe that eventually produced the human species was more convincing as a description of God than Tillich's enigmatic phrase 'being itself': God was not so much the maker of the world or the cause of the evolutionary process; rather, the mysterious process of an evolving universe *was* God. It became clear why the so-called 'process theology' that had originated with the philosopher A. N. Whitehead, was growing ever more popular.

At this same time (1963) appeared Bishop John Robinson's small but explosive book, *Honest to God*. It was considerably more radical than Protestant liberalism, and although readers of Tillich and Bonhoeffer found little new in this book, it alerted the general public to what was going on in some academic circles and soon became the most widely read theological book of the twentieth century.

Already, however, a wave of Christian conservatism was beginning to challenge a declining liberalism. My encounter with this rising tide resulted from a later book by Robinson, *The New Reformation?* The editor of our Presbyterian journal *The Outlook* invited me to write an article for Reformation Sunday. Taking my cue from Robinson, I discussed why a New Reformation in the church had become necessary. "Is the Christian faith inextricably bound up with the world-view of ancient mankind", I asked, "or can the substance of it be translated into the world-view of twentieth-century mankind?" I pointed out that some claims of the sixteenth-century Reformers were simply not true, asserting: "The Bible is not literally inerrant. The Bible is not a simple guide setting forth what every Christian in every generation must be believe and do".

This article raised a few eyebrows, but it would have been quickly forgotten had the editor of *The Outlook* not invited me to write another article for his Easter edition. In this I raised the question of how the claim that Jesus rose from the dead and ascended into heaven can be in conformity with modern concepts of reality. I drew upon a statement by Professor Gregor Smith of Glasgow in his just-published book, *Secular Christianity*. "We may freely say that the bones of Jesus lie somewhere in Palestine. Christian faith is not destroyed by this admission. On the contrary, only now, when this has been said, are we in a position to ask about the meaning of the resurrection as an integral part of the message concerning Jesus".

My article raised a veritable storm. The next issues of *The Outlook* were filled with letters to the editor, some in praise and some in angry and even violent disagreement. Then the newspapers reported that the Auckland Presbytery had met in private to discuss a certain controversial article but its members were bound to secrecy. This made news reporters all the more eager. To meet public demand to know what was behind the secrecy, several metropolitan newspapers then published the offending article in full. What started as a Presbyterian debate quickly became a public donnybrook.

I tried to pour oil on troubled waters by writing four articles for *The Outlook*, explaining the background of the debate. I naively imagined that a short course in current theological thinking would suffice to make people see the whole issue in a different light. Alas, the new articles had a result much like throwing petrol on a blazing fire, and the wrangling quickly spun out of control.

The controversy was deadly serious and at times very heated. A public meeting of Presbyterian men, sponsored by Sir James Fletcher and Sir William Goodfellow and convened in the Auckland Town Hall, established the NZ Association of Presbyterian Laymen for the express purpose of restoring sound doctrine to the Presbyterian Church.

The church's doctrine committee tried to settle the matter by preparing a statement on the resurrection. Eventually approved unanimously by the General Assembly, it affirmed that 'God raised Jesus Christ from the dead in triumph over sin and death

to reign with the Father as sovereign over all'. This drew upon
such traditional language that neither liberal nor radical could
disagree with it. The difficulty was that it simply fudged the issues by failing to address the question of what is meant by the
words 'resurrection from the dead'; and that is what the controversy was really about. That would have ended the matter if it
had been a genuine and honest resolution. Unfortunately, it had
simply papered over the cracks in an attempt to restore church
harmony. Events were soon to show the hollowness of the short-
lived unanimity.

In March 1967 I was invited to preach at the annual inaugural
service of Victoria University. I chose to speak about the book of
Ecclesiastes, which I saw as reflecting many contemporary problems, since it was the work of a Jewish thinker puzzled by what
to make of his religious heritage in relation to the Hellenistic
cultural context of his native Alexandria.

In the course of this sermon I expanded upon my written text
and uttered the words 'Man has no immortal soul'. An enter-
prising journalist in the congregation, sensing another radical
departure from orthodoxy, seized upon this one sentence. After
headlining it in the next morning's news, he telephoned various
church leaders to ask them what they thought. Most claimed
to be totally shocked; apparently they had not been keeping up
with their reading. In academic circles it had long been recognised that the idea of an immortal human soul had come from
the Greek philosophers and not from the Bible. Does not even
the New Testament itself declare that only God is immortal?

My sermon was subsequently published in most newspapers
and produced widespread public discussion on the sensitive issue
of what happens to us when we die. Probably never before or
since were so many people in New Zealand focused on the question of 'life after death'. For weeks, it seemed, the newspapers
carried daily articles on the story, and when news of it reached
Australia, the *Sydney Morning Herald* ran an editorial on the

issue and followed it with a full-page article in their *Weekend Magazine* on whether we humans have immortal souls.

The Laymen's Association called for a special meeting of the General Assembly to defend what they understood as unchangeable Christian beliefs, but their request was eventually declined and the regular November meeting of the Assembly was left to deal with the issue.

But that did not stop the daily newspapers, church journals including the Catholic *Tablet* and *Zealandia*, and secular media from continuing the spate of articles and letters to the editors. I found myself being assailed as everything from the Devil Incarnate to the new Galileo. In most of this I did not recognise myself at all; it was as if two contrary mental images of me had arisen in the collective consciousness of New Zealanders—one hateful and the other honourable.

The storm that swirled around me made me realise that I had touched a very sensitive nerve both in the church and in society. Of course, it could have been anyone; I just happened to be the person who did it. Clearly, the Christian tradition was at a crossroads. The growing tension between traditional Christian thought and academic enquiry had finally reached the breaking point.

Recognising the important implications of this situation, I decided to accept the invitation of Hodder and Stoughton to write a book about it, and over the next six months or so I wrote a chapter every fortnight. I did not examine the topics of resurrection or immortality; that book was to come later. It was first necessary to explain in nonacademic language what lay behind this widespread controversy. That is how I came to write *God in the New World*. Little did I then realise that this would introduce a series of books, several of which included the word 'God' in the title.

The book at hand had to be finished by October, when the General Assembly was to meet to hear the charges of doctrinal error that had been laid against me by two fellow-Presbyterians. One, Bob Blaikie, was a minister with a good theological background; the other was a layman, Robert Wardlaw, who had a very simplistic view of Christianity.

On Friday, 3 November 1967, I was called to the bar of the Assembly to hear the charges presented by my accusers. There was an electric air of expectancy. More than one thousand people packed the church, with an overflow in the hall, and the lamps of the television crews increased the temperature. On Monday I answered the charges, addressing the Assembly for an hour and a half. After lunch the debate began; but before any serious discussion of the real issues could take place, a motion was put to the house and overwhelmingly carried by a voice vote: 'that the Assembly judges no doctrinal error has been established, dismisses the charges, and declares the case closed'.

But despite the Assembly's dismissal of the charges, the divisions that had now become public could not be easily healed. Robert Wardlaw resigned from the church and started one of his own, and a number of individuals transferred to other denominations. The New Zealand press once again devoted editorials to the subject, and even the *London Times* mentioned the case. The Catholic *Zealandia* was impressed by my defence and likened me to Luther, but ended by saying, "Where does this leave the Presbyterian church now that it has sold Christianity down the river?" That of course was yet to be determined. The *NZ Weekly News* devoted a lead article to the question, declaring, 'The church will never be the same again'. In many ways it was right.

I had embraced the Christian faith in 1937, and now thirty years later the year 1967 marked the second turning point in my religious life. Like many others I had come to regard the church as a holy society, manifesting a special quality of life. It came as a great shock to discover that behind its benign face it could also harbour poisonous thoughts and sheer hatred, even in those who claimed to be its most zealous guardians. The sad realisation that despite its many fine members the church is as human as any other society made me feel shame for the institution.

Soon after *God in the New World* was published in April 1968, one well-known newspaper printed on the same page two reviews reflecting completely antithetical opinions. A former Moderator of the Presbyterian Church said the book 'explains the real nature of the Bible', while the editor of the Catholic *Tablet* said 'this book sweeps away Christian belief'.

My chapter on God ends with these words: 'By God-talk we are pointing to the deepest reality we can encounter, to that which concerns us ultimately. But we do not know what that is. The God that is known is an idol. The God who can be defined is no God. It is of the essence of human existence that we live not by knowledge but by faith. It is by faith that we are led to fulfilment and our ultimate destiny, and God is the ground of our faith.'

Of course the controversy that preceded the publication helped to make the book a best seller, and having now become a public figure, I was invited to contribute to a series of monographs designed for use in seventh forms. Mine was entitled, *God in the Twentieth Century,* and in it I spoke of the history of the word 'God', why it had to be treated as a symbolic word, and why one had to learn the most appropriate ways to use the symbol, just as in mathematics one had to learn how to use and not to use the symbol for infinity.

Yet otherwise the next three years of my life went on as usual. I set about researching and writing a book on the topic that had ignited the extraordinary controversy—the Resurrection. In it I showed that far from denoting a miraculous event of cosmic proportions, the idea of resurrection, an idiomatic or symbolic expression of hope, had a long history. It was a concept that arose from observing the earth's yearly resuscitation in spring after its wintry death. Later, in Ezekiel's famous vision of the valley of dry bones, it became a metaphor for the rebirth of the people of Israel. Only 150 years before the Christian era it was being applied to the Jewish martyrs in the Maccabean Revolt; and finally it was applied to Jesus after his crucifixion by the Romans to express the hope that his martyrdom also would not be in vain. And it was a resurrection affirmed by an account of visions and the legend of a tomb found empty.

But before this book was published in 1971 I had already left the Theological Hall. I realised that I had become a kind of marked man, and conservative forces in the church were ready to pounce on the slightest provocation. Because of remarks in a television interview I gave in Brisbane in 1970, they persuaded the General Assembly to dissociate itself from my views. No doubt many in the church heaved a sigh of relief when, three weeks later, the Victoria University of Wellington made me the first Professor of Religious Studies in any New Zealand University. I entered an atmosphere of intellectual freedom and calm I had not felt for some time, and welcomed the opportunity to return to the wider field of religious studies.

The recent theological controversy led me to choose the phenomenon of religious change in the modern secular world as my chief area of research. Accordingly, I instituted a second-year course, entitled 'Religion in Change', for which I wrote a textbook published in 1981 as *Faith's New Age*.[1]

I concluded that in modern times humankind has entered a cultural world vastly different from those during which the great religious traditions of the world were founded. The major part of the book therefore traces this change, step by step, from the late Middle Ages onwards. The book as whole, however, is structured according to the three successive cultural periods through which humankind has lived, and in the context of which the diversity of human religious experience can be more clearly understood.

To begin with, I constructed this paradigm on the basis of Karl Jaspers' idea of an Axial Period consisting of a few centuries on either side of 500 BCE. He observed that it was during this period that in some five different places in Asia there arose quite independently from each other prophets, thinkers, and philosophers who dared to question the cultures they had inherited. We know them as Zarathustra, the Buddha, Confucius, the Israelite prophets and the Greek philosophers. They founded the great religious traditions—Zoroastrianism, Buddhism, Jainism, classical Hinduism, Confucianism and Judaism, the last of which later led to Christianity and Islam. I combined this insight with Robert Bellah's seminal essay 'Religious Evolution', and have found the resulting concept of three great cultural periods so illuminating and helpful that it has informed all my later books.

The first cultural period I have called the Ethnic Phase, for it was a time when each of the many independent cultures evolved out of its ethnic identity and served to perpetuate it. In this phase of cultural evolution no distinction was made between religion and culture or between morality and ritual. People saw themselves living in a world controlled by gods and spirits that personified the forces of nature. These forces were often fickle and immoral, but they had to be obeyed and placated.

Next came the Axial Period that ushered in what I have called the Transethnic Phase, in which ethnic identity was relegated to a secondary place. Religion and culture now came to be distinguished from each other, as did ritual and morality. This enabled the post-Axial religions to cross ethnic boundaries. The three most successful were Buddhism, Christianity and Islam, which by the year 1900 had more or less divided the globe into the Buddhist Orient, the Islamic Middle East and the Christian West.

Already, however, a second Axial Divide had emerged. This time it appeared only in Western Europe, but it has given rise to a third phase of cultural evolution that may be called global. Whereas the first was ethnic and polytheistic and the second transethnic and theological, the third is global and humanistic.

This modern humanistic culture is now spreading all around the globe. It is undermining all traditional forms of religion, including the Christianity from which it evolved. It is also triggering reactionary religious movements of a fundamentalist nature in Christianity, Islam and Hinduism. All of these vigorously reject the new humanistic and secular culture, and each seeks to restore and preserve its own past.

In *Faith's New Age* I tried to show that while the modern world is sounding the death knell of the traditional religions, it is at the same time heralding new manifestations of what it means to be religious. Religious thought and endeavour must now fasten its attention on *this world* rather than on *otherworldly* goals, and therefore can properly be called secular—not in the sense of meaning 'nonreligious' or 'antireligious', but simply 'this-worldly'. In this new cultural age we are becoming aware of how much all humans have in common irrespective of class, race, religion, gender or age. We are developing a growing concern for human rights, and are coming to see that what used to be regarded as divine or transcendent absolutes are actually human judgments that express what our forebears found to be of ultimate concern to them.

As a result of this cultural map of our cultural evolution, I went on to write in 1994 *Tomorrow's God*. Traditionally, our forebears believed that it was God who created both us and the world, and that he did so for a discoverable purpose of his design. This book sketches the evolution of human culture and religion by showing how by words, ideas and stories we humans have slowly created the many and various worlds of meaning in which we live and move and have our being. We are all born into a cultural world of meaning inherited from our ancestors. It shapes us, and we in turn help to reshape it as we pass it on to our children. To say, as we have long done, that 'we were created by God' is to be blind to the fact that we humans created the word 'God' along with language, culture, religion and science.

Once this was understood, it became possible to write *A History of God*, as the former nun Karen Armstrong has done so brilliantly in her best-seller of that name. I myself have similarly sketched the history of 'God', showing how the concept was created by human imagination in the ancient pre-Axial past, where it referred to a class of invisible spiritual beings associated with the forces of nature.

But during the first Axial Period these gods were critically examined and largely abandoned. For example, the same Israelite prophets who declared they had no real existence retained the collective term for them—*elohim*—but gave the plural word a new meaning. By referring to God (*Elohim*) as 'the One', the one who created and gave meaning to everything, they gave birth to monotheism. 'The LORD our God is One', say the Jews; 'Allah is *Al Wahid* (the One)', say the Muslims.

Christians inherited monotheism from the Jews but developed the God idea a stage further. Because of their veneration of the man known as Jesus of Nazareth, they said God had come down to dwell among us and had taken on human flesh. And then for good measure, through their doctrine of the Holy Spirit, they incorporated human consciousness into their understanding of God. Thus originated the doctrine of the Holy Trinity.

This doctrine made Christianity unique and served it well for some fifteen hundred years. Only in the second Axial Period did this doctrine, along with the whole edifice of Christian dogma, begin to disintegrate. One of the first to realise what was happening was Friedrich Nietzsche, who in his famous parable of the madman (c. 1880) announced that the idea of god was now dead. Some seventy years later a number of radical Christian theologians also declared that 'God is dead'.

Does this also mean the death of Christianity? Many assume that to be the case, since the one thing on which atheists and traditional Christians agree is that Christianity presupposes belief in a personal God who created and continues to control the world. I do not agree with this assumption, for as I have tried to show in *Christianity without God*, two crucial developments intervened. Not only did the Jewish tradition undergo a radical change in giving rise to the Judeo-Christian tradition, but before the 'death of God' was proclaimed, it underwent a further radical change during the second Axial Period, and is now evolving into the Judeo-Christian-humanistic tradition that has given birth to the modern humanistic and global world.

I recently delivered a lecture to the Royal Society in Wellington, in which I explored what lay behind a statement by the German physicist, Friedrich von Weizsäcker: 'Modern science would not perhaps have been possible without Christianity'. We do well to ponder what he then went on to say: 'The church is blind to the true nature of modern times; the modern world is equally blind to its own nature. Both are blind to the significance of secularisation. The modern world was the result of the secularisation of Christianity'.

Of course, this modern world is no longer Christian in the traditional sense, but neither is it anti-Christian. It holds in high regard the moral values, aspirations and social goals it has inherited from its Christian matrix. It is the logical development of the doctrine of the incarnation, of God becoming enfleshed in the human condition.

Not too long ago I was delivering a lecture to some two hundred alumni of Auckland University, many of them medical graduates. I was assigned the topic 'Playing God'. This was meant to reflect the fact that we humans have now reached the point in our cultural and religious evolution where we are now required to make decisions which previously we assumed to be within the exclusive province of God. In numerous activities of special breeding, for example, we have been doing it for some time, but now we are gaining control over the very creation of new life and matters of life and death: contraception, in vitro fertilisation, genetic modification, cloning and euthanasia. Indeed, we occasionally determine, often unthinkingly, what species will survive or become extinct.

Are we humans ready for these heavy responsibilities? Probably not! But ready or not, these responsibilities are now on our shoulders. That is why in *The World to Come*, a book I wrote in 1999, I took up the painful obligation of sketching some very frightening scenarios of what may occur during the twenty-first century. They graphically illustrate why our first obligation is do our best to gain a clear understanding of the cultural times in which we live, and how we got here. After that, we must glean what wisdom we can from the past in order to help us make wise decisions for the future.

My 2004 book *Is Christianity Going Anywhere?* acknowledges that we have come to the end of traditional Christianity, indicates the new phase into which it has already entered, and suggests that our rediscovery of the footprints and voiceprints of the original Jesus can help us and inspire us on the way ahead.

During my lifetime I have seen and experienced great religious change. That is why first in my preaching, then in my teaching and finally in my writing I have tried to interpret this change as clearly and as honestly as I could. I find myself living in a new and ever-changing world, but I have been intrigued to discover that much of what I have learned about our Christian past suddenly sparkles with new meaning. Therefore, I conclude this account of 'God and me' with the words of the medieval Christian mystic Meister Eckhart (1260–1327): 'The eye with which I see God, and the eye with which God sees me are one and the same eye'.

Footnote

1. A revised version of this book was published by Polebridge Press in 2001 as *Christian Faith at the Crossroads*.

CHAPTER 2

The Faith
to Doubt

To explore the topic of faith and doubt, one must first define the very important distinction to be made between faith and belief, then turn to the relationship of faith and doubt, and finally suggest what it may mean to say, 'I believe in God'.

The general public today tends to imagine that religious faith consists of holding a certain number of specific and often irrational beliefs. It is particularly in connection with Christianity that this perception is most widely to be found, and unfortunately it is often strongly promoted by the churches themselves. At a very early stage Christian conviction came to be referred to as 'the faith' and this subsequently led to the identification of faith with giving assent to a set of unchangeable beliefs, referred to as the creeds or standard Christian doctrines. These doctrines came to be regarded as absolute and unchangeable on the grounds that they had been revealed by God, the source of all truth. Of course, that conviction itself is simply another belief that underlies the rest.

As Wilfred Cantwell Smith, an American scholar of international repute, pointed out, the perception that faith consists in holding a certain set of beliefs is actually quite a modern phenomenon. He put it this way: "The idea that believing is

First presented to the Sea of Faith Network (NZ) Conference 1997, and subsequently published in *The Lloyd Geering Reader*, eds. Paul Morris and Mike Grimshaw (Victoria University Press, 2007).

religiously important turns out to be a modern idea. . . . The great modern heresy of the church is the heresy of believing. Not of believing this or that but of believing as such. The view that to believe is of central significance—this is an aberration".

To put the matter in blunt and overly simplistic terms, we may say that in premodern times people put their faith in God, whereas today too many put their faith in such beliefs as the inerrancy of the Bible. This modern error of equating faith with holding certain beliefs began to develop in the nineteenth century. That is why Lewis Carroll poked fun at it in 1865 when he wrote *Alice in Wonderland*. There he portrayed Alice as saying, "I can't possibly believe that!"—to which the Queen replied, "Perhaps you haven't had enough practice. Why, I have believed as many as six impossible things before breakfast". To identify faith with the holding of a certain number of beliefs that come to us from the distant past actually makes a mockery of Christian faith and reduces it to the schoolboy's definition: "Faith is believing things you know ain't true".

To begin with, it is necessary to recognise how easily we can be and often have been misled by the way language changes over the centuries, and to recall that language is basic to the human condition. We are all products of language-based cultures, and every religion is clothed in a specific language and expressed in a particular set of verbal symbols. This is one important reason why the medieval Western church was reluctant to allow the Bible to be translated into the vernacular, and why Islam refuses to accept any translation of the Qur'an from the original Arabic. But more of that later.

Wilfred Cantwell Smith wrote two books, *Belief and History* and *Faith and Belief*, in which he meticulously traces the radical changes that have taken place in the meaning attached to such words as 'belief' and 'faith'. These books, which should be required reading in every theological college, show how our words 'belief' and 'faith' have changed in meaning since earlier times. When people today say 'I believe in God', they are often simply expressing their opinion or conviction that there exists a spiritual being called God. But that is not what people meant by 'belief in God' four centuries ago. To be sure, it was their common conviction that a supernatural being called God had created and continued to control the world. But to them that seemed so self-evident, that it did not have to be spelled out. When they said 'I believe in God', they were saying something much more than that.

The difference between their use of the word 'believe' and ours can be best illustrated by noting that some people today will say they 'believe in the Devil'. No medieval Christian would have dreamed of saying such a dreadful thing. Of course it was their opinion that the Devil existed, but to say 'I believe in the Devil' in those days meant giving one's allegiance to the devil. The appropriate expression would have been not 'I believe in the Devil', but 'I renounce the devil'—meaning 'I will reject all suggestions made to me by the Devil'. Similarly, 'I believe in God' did not mean 'It is my opinion that a God exists', but rather 'I give my allegiance to God' or 'I entrust myself to God'. Obviously, it would have been unthinkable to say, 'I entrust myself to the Devil'.

This earlier meaning of 'believe' is also apparent from its roots in Latin, which of course was the universal language of Western medieval Christendom. The Latin word *credo*, which also gives us the word creed, was translated in English as 'I believe' and its etymology is very revealing. It is made up from *do* (I give) and *cor* (heart). Originally, '*credo*' meant 'I give my heart to'. The Latin word for 'believe', as we now understand that word, was *opinor*, which gives us our word 'opinion'.

Thus, as the Oxford English Dictionary explains, "*belief* was the earlier word for what is now commonly called *faith*". 'Belief in God' used to mean 'putting one's trust in God', but it now refers to an opinion about reality—for instance, that the world was created by and is ruled by a supernatural personal being.

This belief, like all beliefs, is human in origin and expression; and not only do human beliefs and opinions continually change as cultures develop, but this particular belief has never been universal to all humankind. And in the Western world, where it was once practically universal, it is now held by increasingly fewer people. In medieval times no one questioned the existence of unseen spiritual beings, because such a realm seemed eminently self-evident. The supreme being they called God, but just as real to them were angels, spirits, and the Devil, whose existence they did not think to question, since these were all part of the belief structure that formed the medieval view of reality. At stake, then, was not what one believed (in our sense of the word 'belief'), but in which of these self-evident beings did one place one's ultimate trust? That is what they meant by saying 'I believe in God'.

It is because we live in a cultural setting so different from either the ancient or the medieval worlds that these previously common beliefs no longer have the power to convince us. To commit oneself to the beliefs of former generations can be spiritually harmful and may even become a form of idolatry. To regard any set of beliefs as absolute and unchangeable is to make an idol of something that is human, finite, and fallible. We should accept the beliefs of others or those from the past only if they have the inherent power to convince us. This topic is taken up in more detail in Chapter 10.

In the last four hundred years, and particularly in the nineteenth and twentieth centuries, culture and the general knowledge upon which it is founded have been changing rapidly. Therefore people's beliefs have been changing. Less than two hundred years ago nearly everybody in the Western world believed the earth was only six thousand years old, and that we were all descended from two common ancestors, Adam and Eve. Those are only two of a great number of beliefs universally held by Christians before 1800 but no longer entertained by well-informed people today, not even by most Christians.

Because such outmoded beliefs had long been woven into the language and concepts by which former generations expressed their faith, far too many assumed that to walk the Christian path of faith one had to accept the same beliefs as earlier Christians. The confusion of the words 'belief' and 'faith' as they are used in the creeds only served to support this false assumption. The church itself must acknowledge some of the blame for this error.

In any place and time, the beliefs that people hold depend on the culture that has shaped them, their own particular experience, and their personal reflection on both. If we had lived in the Middle Ages we would almost certainly have believed that the earth was flat, and probably that the stars were the lights of heaven. We might well have believed that if we could rise high enough into the sky, we would see God on his golden throne surrounded by angels. As Cantwell Smith says, "One's beliefs belong to the century one lives in".

Faith, however, is something altogether different. There were people of faith in the Middle Ages. There are people of faith today. But the body of beliefs held by people at different times and from within which they attempt to express that faith in words may differ very considerably.

To recover the full significance of faith demands that we divorce it from any notion of commitment to particular beliefs. This may be illustrated by showing how faith is related to doubt, the experience of which has too often been misunderstood and undervalued in Christian circles. This misapprehension likely owed something to the gospel account of Doubting Thomas and later to John Bunyan's famous allegory, *The Pilgrim's Progress*, in which he described Giant Despair dwelling in Doubting Castle.

To be sure, the absence of faith can be described as despair; but the absence of doubt is not faith but credulity—a very different thing indeed.

Actually, the capacity to doubt plays a very important role in both personal and cultural growth. When we are children we cherish such beliefs as the existence of fairies and elves, and the yearly visit of Santa Claus. But if beyond a certain age we continue to confuse them with the real world, our notions will be seen as childish. The time comes when we must put such fancies behind us and move on. As St Paul rightly observed, "When I was a child I thought like a child. I reasoned like a child. But when I became a man I gave up my childish ways".

What enables us to put fantasy behind us and grow to maturity is the capacity to doubt. When a child of six or seven begins to doubt Saint Nick's ability to get down the chimney or to be in so many different places at once, then he or she begins to doubt the objective reality of this mysterious person. The same capacity to doubt emerges during the often turbulent period of adolescence. We first doubt and then challenge the validity of our parent's authority. We come to recognise that these once authoritative and almost divine figures are quite human and fallible after all. The perplexing process of alternating between doubt and trust, rebellion and obedience, is essential for our growth to mature adulthood. Persons of fifty who still rely on their parents for guidance in everyday matters are clearly suffering from stunted growth.

And so it is with the evolution of culturally defined opinions. Without the capacity to doubt, we cannot grow from childish beliefs to the maturity of faith. Doubt is not the enemy of faith, but of false beliefs. Indeed, our entire catalogue of assumptions and beliefs should be continually subjected to critical examination, and those found to be false or inadequate should be replaced by those we find convincing within our cultural context.

Yet expressing or even entertaining doubt sometimes takes so much courage that we may say it takes real faith to doubt.

Thirty years ago an anonymous well-wisher sent me through the post a little book entitled *The Faith to Doubt* by the American scholar Homes Hartshorne. I found it an exciting text and have treasured it ever since. Among other things it says, "People today are not in need of assurances about the truth of doubtful beliefs. They need the faith to doubt. They need the faith by which to reject idols. The churches cannot preach to this age if they stand outside of it, living in the illusory security of yesterday's beliefs. These [already] lie about us broken, and we cannot by taking thought raise them from the dead".

Far from demonstrating a lack of faith, the very act of discarding outworn beliefs may in fact do just the opposite by opening the door for genuine faith to operate again. Indeed the assertion that one needs to believe a particular creed or set of doctrines in order to have faith is an invitation to credulity rather than to faith—and childlike faith is vastly different from childish credulity.

Neither is faith reached by the path of logical argument and convincing evidence. Those are the ways by which we test our beliefs. But faith rests not on proof, but on conviction. We see this in the story of doubting Thomas, who said, "Unless I see in his hands the print of the nails and place my finger in the mark of the nails and place my hand in his side, I cannot have faith". Jesus' reply to that was, "Blessed are those who have not seen and yet have faith". In other words, they are blessed who have faith without asking for any proof. Faith that requires proof or demonstration is no faith at all. In fact, anyone who tries to defend the truth of Christianity by proving it thereby shows lack of faith.

Does this mean that we are free to believe anything we like? Yes and no! First let us note that our beliefs are not embraced by choice. That is why people sometimes say, 'I cannot possibly believe that!' Rather our beliefs take shape as a result of our experience and the impact of our cultural tradition upon us. But we must be left free from the constraints of external authority to formulate beliefs that do not violate our honesty and integrity. We rightly resist having other people's beliefs imposed upon us, for that would be tantamount to intellectual slavery. If we settle for simply repeating the creeds of former generations as our own, we allow ourselves to be turned into ventriloquists' dummies.

But while we should be free to allow experience to determine our beliefs, it does not follow that what we believe is of no consequence. To believe that one can jump off a high cliff without coming to any harm could be very dangerous. And as the Jonestown tragedy illustrates, it is possible to hold very dangerous religious beliefs. The benefit of subjecting our beliefs to critical examination powerfully attests the importance of doubt: it both delivers us from dangerous beliefs and opens the door to genuine faith.

As soon as we disjoin faith from some of the now outmoded beliefs traditionally associated with Christianity we come to see that the Christian tradition has no monopoly on faith. Indeed, faith is far more inclusive and widespread than any particular set of beliefs and practices. This is why Jesus was able to commend the trust he found in certain Gentiles who clearly did not share his Jewish beliefs.

Faith is a quality of human living. Nearly everybody has some faith, however limited its breadth or depth. "Everywhere, and at all times humans have lived by faith, both individually and corporately", said Cantwell Smith. To have no faith is to be in a condition of absolute despair, to find no meaning or significance in anything, to feel that life is not worth the candle. If such a condition persists for long our physical health soon deteriorates and we die—or in extreme cases we may take our own life.

Any division of humanity, then, is not a case of separating people into those who have faith and those who have none; it is rather a matter of their having great faith or only a little. And of course through life our faith may ebb and flow according to the changing circumstances in which we live. As human beings we are all born with the capacity and the need for faith; one need only note that even from infancy children have a natural inclination to respond in trust to those around them. Today, many adults are finding it necessary to move to the margins of traditional Christian orthodoxy in order to rediscover a genuine faith—one that is much more than words and beliefs, one that can never be adequately expressed in words, one that is the positive response of the whole person to life, that involves the emotions and the will just as much as the mind.

Faith may begin as the trustful response of infancy, but the way we grow in faith is quite complex. For faith is caught rather than taught. We catch it from others—our parents, our friends, our peers, our teachers, the people we work with, and the people we come to admire. People of faith are a great boon to society for they foster faith in others and inspire them with trust and hope. We feel drawn to people of great faith, for perhaps even more unconsciously than consciously we sense that they have something we need, and that some of it may rub off on us.

Many different elements of our experience and cultural environment serve to nurture faith. After all, that is the role of verbal symbols and belief systems in a particular culture. All the great religious traditions originated from men and women of great faith, vision, and hope—inspiring leaders who through the centuries have enabled people to walk the path of faith. For of course Christianity is not the only such path, a fact acknowledged in the title of one of the standard textbooks we used to use in religious studies classes. It was called simply *Paths of Faith*.

Thus the closest synonym of faith is not belief, but trust. Faith is a total response of trust towards the world in general, towards people, and towards the future; and it has a strong affinity with hope. This is reflected in the letter to the Hebrews, "Faith is the assurance of things hoped for", and in the famous hymn in which Paul coupled it with hope in his trinity of the eternal virtues—faith, hope, and love.

Faith also involves integrity, or wholeness; it disavows intellectual contradiction and moral inconsistency. Claiming beliefs that you secretly doubt undermines faith instead of promoting it, for it means that you are at cross-purposes with yourself. On this point, one might well consider the well-known verse from the prophet Habakkuk that is commonly translated, "The just shall live by his faith". A better translation is, "The righteous man shall live by reason of his integrity". The word translated as 'faith' or 'integrity' has to do with steadfastness, fidelity, reliability. It comes from the same verbal root as the word 'Amen', and is the concept that underlies all references to faith in the New Testament.

It is also reflected in the words of Jesus to the woman who clutched at his garment in the hope of being made well. When she found herself healed, he said to her, "It is your faith that has made you whole". He did not mean for one moment that she had the right beliefs. He was referring to her attitude of trust, fidelity, and inner steadfastness or integrity.

Our Christian cultural heritage will continue as a viable path of communal faith in today's global village only if it leaves us free to believe what we find personally convincing and at the same inspires us to walk into the unknown future with hope and faith.

It is just such a model of faith we find in Abraham. Whatever his beliefs, they were certainly very different from ours. He knew nothing about Moses and the Torah, yet he is honoured by Jews as their spiritual father. He knew nothing about the Qur'an but is honoured by Islam as the first Muslim. He knew nothing about Jesus Christ and the so-called Christian Gospel, yet the first Christians honoured him as the very model of a man of faith. "By faith Abraham obeyed when he was called to go out to a place which he was to receive as an inheritance; and he went out not knowing where he was to go".

The story of Abraham as the model of a person of faith transcends all the different beliefs found in these three traditions and pinpoints what seems to be essential to faith. But it still leaves us with a problem. Since Abraham is said to have obeyed God, does it follow that some kind of belief in God or belief about God is essential to faith in the modern sense of the word? In turning now to this question we shall also be dealing with another that is often posed: 'It is all very well to talk about faith as trust, but in what or in whom are we to put our trust?' The short answer to this latter question is that in the monotheistic traditions the answer has always been understood and verbally expressed as 'God'. But this very fact shows how culturally insular we have become. Buddhism is a path of faith that from its beginning abandoned the concept of God or the gods. Confucianism is a path of faith, but Chinese has no word for God. Therefore, the first Christian missionaries to China, needing a verbal symbol for their Deity, chose an already existing Chinese word and gave it a new meaning. Unfortunately the Protestants chose one word and the Roman Catholics chose another. The embarrassing confusion that naturally ensued is a powerful reminder of how much religious understanding and indeed our humanity depend on language—a human creation that we inherit from the past where it slowly evolved, and that is still evolving.

In point of fact, the evolution of language is the key to human culture in general and to religion in particular—a topic I have explored at some length in *Tomorrow's God*. At birth we enter a language-based culture that both nurtures the development of our individual consciousness and powerfully shapes the way we see reality.

As Don Cupitt has well said, "Language is the medium in which we live and move and have our being. In it we act, we structure the world, and order every aspect of our social life. Only Language stands between us and the Void. It shapes everything".

Every human culture—and indeed human existence itself—is based on language. Every religious tradition depends on a language for its expression and cognitive understanding. In monotheistic cultures the most basic word, the one that undergirds all the rest, is the word 'God'. But where did this word come from, and why? Until modern times few people paused even to ponder the question. In the cultural context that obtained until recently, people had every reason to believe that human knowledge of God went back to the time of Adam and Eve, only a few thousand years ago.

Only in the last few centuries have we been able to show that the word 'God', the very concept of God, and indeed all concepts, are only creations of the human mind, but have a long and fascinating history. One of the clearest demonstrations of this can be found in Karen Armstrong's book, *A History of God*.

Since this is hardly the time to trace that history, it must suffice to point out that the word 'god' originated in ancient cultures to indicate one of a class of invisible beings by which to explain the phenomena people observed in a natural world full of mystery and wonder. The gods thus came to birth as the creation of the collective human mind. The process of conceiving and naming the gods, all made possible through language, was a way of ordering their world and providing a rational explanation for whatever they observed and encountered in nature. To note but two familiar examples, they referred to the sky as father (still reflected in the words 'our heavenly Father') and the earth as mother (and we still speak of 'Mother Nature'!).

As we attempt to envisage the birth of the gods from a cultural context that has long abandoned primitive polytheism, we too often fail to appreciate that the 'gods' were just as much concepts of primitive 'science' (that is, knowledge of reality) as they were of primitive religion. Where modern physicists coin such terms as electrons, quarks and black holes in order to explain natural phenomena, the ancients coined such terms as spirits, jinn, angels, devils and gods. We now regard the ancient gods as imaginary figures, because they are not part of the way we understand the world. For the ancients, however, they were very real figures indeed.

The time came, however, when the objective reality of these personifications began to be questioned. That is how the human capacity to doubt brought about the next stage in cultural growth in the long human path of faith. At first doubt was openly expressed only by a few very brave souls, but from their pioneering thinking some two and a half thousand years ago emerged the new and fruitful paths of faith we call the great world religions.

There we find a very interesting thing happening to the concept of the gods. The Chinese version, if such had existed, dropped out of use. In Buddhism the idea of god was deliberately bypassed. In both Greece and Israel the notion of god was retained but quite radically transformed, when the many gods were replaced by one God, and this symbolic word continued to perform the religious role of representing the centre of a meaningful world.

Plato's *God* was the essence of goodness, the creative source of everything, the universal, impersonal, and eternal 'form' behind the humanly conceived gods of Olympus. For Aristotle God was even less personal than for Plato, being chiefly conceived as the Prime Mover of the cosmic system. The Stoics, in turn, conceived God as the principle of rationality and order that pervades all things.

The ideas of these Greek thinkers were later to have a profound influence on the Christian understanding of God, but in the process they became synthesised with another tradition, whose transformation had simultaneously taken place in the tiny nation of Israel at the instigation of their prophets. In that case, the 'gods' as a class of beings were scornfully banished from reality in favour of one supreme invisible spirit known only through speech, a transition that took place in stages over several centuries.

It is important to observe that in spite of their demolition of 'the gods' as a class of beings, the Israelites retained the Hebrew word for 'the gods', *elohim* (still plural in form), but gave it a new connotation, just as the Greek philosophers had done with *theos*. The word has two referents in the Old Testament: when it refers to the gods of the nations it has a plural meaning, but when it refers to Yahweh it is understood as singular.

Thus in the Hebrew Bible, 'God' is sometimes a proper name and sometimes not. We frequently find the word *elohim* attached to people—as in 'the god of Israel', 'the god of Abraham', 'my god', 'your god'. And increasingly we see the word used in a symbolic way to refer to whatever values a person or a nation treated as supreme. For example, if you were to ask, 'Where shall I find the god of Abraham?', the appropriate answer would be, 'Observe how Abraham lives his life. Look for what he regards to be of ultimate worth; that is all you will ever know of the god of Abraham. His "god" consists of the values he lives by, the voice he seeks to obey and the goals he hopes to achieve.'

What eventuated as the classical Christian understanding of God owed almost as much to Aristotle, the Stoics, and especially Plato as it did to the Israelite prophets. The transcendental, otherworldly, unchanging God of Plato was united in uneasy tension with the immanent, this-worldly, history-guiding God of Israel. The merger was prevented from falling apart by the formulation of the symbolic doctrines of the trinity and the in-carnation. Strangely enough, modern philosophers of religion who defend traditional Christian theism often completely ignore these two doctrines, and are thus left defending the God of Plato and Aristotle rather more than the biblical concept of God.

In Western theism the break with Plato began a long time ago with the Franciscan theologian William of Ockham, who initiated the philosophical tradition known as nominalism. He denied that Plato's universal ideas or 'forms' had any objective reality; they were simply names, he said. They were words or concepts invented by the human mind. Since, for Plato, 'God' was just such a form or name, William of Ockham argued that 'God' likewise had no objective existence, but was simply a name invented by humans. Of course William of Ockham never put it that bluntly or he would have been burnt at the stake, but he pioneered the tradition which was to develop in such later thinkers as Luther, Feuerbach, and Don Cupitt.

Luther showed himself a nominalist when he said,

> A god is that to which we look for all good; to have a god is simply to trust in one with our whole heart . . . the confidence and faith of the heart alone make both god and an idol. If your faith and confidence are right, then likewise your god is the true god. On the other hand, if your confidence is false, then you have not the true god. . . . Whatever your heart clings to and confides in, that is really your god.

Already we find in the phrases "a god is that to which we look for the good" and "whatever your heart clings to and confides in, that is really your god", an acknowledgement of how subjectively the term "god" was coming to be understood. It is not surprising, therefore, that the nineteenth-century theologian and philosopher Ludwig Feuerbach (1804–72)[1] should express quite boldly the implications of Ockham's nominalism by asserting that 'God' is a humanly created concept. Feuerbach concluded that 'God' was an unconscious objectification of all that the human mind felt to be of worth. 'God' had been created in the human imagination as a symbolic amalgam of our highest ideals, aspirations, and values: "By his God you know the man, and by the man his God; the two are identical."

'God' is a verbal symbol, humanly created. All talk and discussion about God (theo-logy means god-talk), said Feuerbach, is really an exercise in human self-understanding. By referring to the God-symbol we are discussing the meaning of human existence. 'God' is the symbol most central or basic to meaning. In the long history of the word 'God', Feuerbach's thinking marked a turning point as radically significant as those marked by the Israelite prophets and the Greek philosophers.

At last we have reached the point where we can acknowledge that 'God' is a word—to be sure, a very important symbolic word—that has no external referent subject to public confirmation. The word 'God' has become a functional term whose content depends on what we (subjectively) put into it, and this process, we have seen, had its beginnings in the Bible, where the prophets denied the objective reality of the gods but retained the word 'God', for that to which Israel should give its allegiance.

The word 'God' performs a very important function in our reflections on the nature of human existence, but its content or meaning is something we must supply. The content with which we invest it is the set of values and aspirations that we acknowledge to have moral and spiritual claims on us—or, if one prefers, the supreme values and goals to which to which we feel ourselves drawn.

The way this content differs from person to person may be clearly illustrated by the fact that while at the collective level Jews, Christians, and Muslims all claim to be monotheists, they cannot be said to worship the same God. The only criterion we have for determining the identity of God are the 'attributes' of God. These attributes constitute the content of the word 'God' and we humans are the ones who determine and enunciate what those attributes are. To Jews, for example, God is the One who delivered their forebears from slavery and gave them the land of Israel. To Christians, God is the One who became incarnate in Jesus Christ. To Muslims, God is the One who appointed Muhammad as the last of his prophets and through whom he delivered the Qur'an. In each case the attribute is a *sine qua non* of the tradition in question, yet in no way can it be reconciled with the others. Indeed, the word 'God' has never had one fixed meaning for all people.

The seminal Jewish philosopher Martin Buber, who in his younger days had been greatly influenced by Feuerbach, wrote a book called *The Eclipse of God* in which he recognized that from modern times onward the word 'God' could no longer mean what it had commonly meant in the past. Yet he still saw an essential use for the word and therefore spoke of the idea of God as being temporarily eclipsed. In the beginning of this book he described his meeting with an elderly Jew whom he refers to as 'a noble old thinker' with whom Buber was staying while visiting another university to lecture to some theology students. The man asked Buber to read to him some of his lecture. When he finished, the old man said, "How can you bring yourself to say 'God' time after time? What word of human speech is so misused, so defiled, so desecrated as this! All the innocent blood that has been shed for it has robbed it of its radiance. All the injustice that it has been used to cover has effaced its features". Buber remarked that the man's kindly eyes flamed with emotion and indignation. They sat together in silence for some time before Buber replied, "Yes, it is the most heavy-laden of all human words. None has become so soiled, so mutilated. Just for this reason I may not abandon it. Generations of people have laid the burden of their anxious lives upon this word. . . . Where might I find a word like it to describe the highest! . . . We cannot cleanse the word 'God' and we cannot make it whole; but defiled and mutilated as it is, we can raise it from the ground and set it over an hour of great care". The old man stood up, laid his hands on Buber's shoulder and said, "Let us be friends". Buber completed the story by adding, "The conversation was completed. For where two or three are truly together, they are together in the name of God".

Whether any of us continues to use the word god or not has now become a matter of personal choice. But this is so with all the vocabulary of the language we use. It is not necessary for us to use the word 'God', not even in order to talk about faith. And if we do use the word, we open ourselves to misunderstanding and confusion. In spite of that, I am inclined like Buber to keep on using it.

If we want to use one word in order to refer to that in which persons of faith put their trust, 'God' is still as good a word as any. But all must be free to spell out for themselves just what that word contains for them. It certainly does not mean for me what it meant for the ancients, including even Jesus of Nazareth, or what it meant for the medievalists or even what it means for traditional theists of today. I do not believe, for example, that the word is the name of a spiritual being who planned and created this universe and who keeps it in his control. What I have learned about this universe suggests to me that it operates as much by chance as by any kind of design. My own existence and the particular DNA formula which makes up the unique physiology of my physical body are themselves the result of a chance meeting of a particular ovum with a particular sperm.

It is my belief that there is no ultimate meaning or purpose permeating this universe, amazing and mysterious though it is. The universe simply is as it is. If we wish to find any meaning during the short time any of us is here, we have to create that meaning for ourselves. And we create the meaning of our lives by the way we live. For me 'God' is a useful symbol, inherited from the past, to refer to that meaning and to those values I find to be supreme, and to those goals I feel myself called to aspire. So when I say 'I believe in God', I mean something like this: 'God is the symbol that holds together in a unity all my bits of knowledge about the world and all the virtues I have come to value, such as love, justice, compassion'. The more I respond positively to all this and learn to trust my fellow humans and the world at large, the more I find human existence to be of great worth and meaningful. Surprisingly, perhaps, I find much of the language of the Bible and the Christian tradition is still very helpful to me. For God, as I understand this word, is to be found in people, in human relationships, in my own thinking, in the mystery of all living creatures, and in the stars and distant nebulae. So when I say 'I believe in God', I mean a whole bundle of things, chief among them such things as these:

I trust my fellow humans.
I trust the world.
I say 'Yes!' to life.
I look forward to each new day in hope and faith.

Footnote

1. For a fuller discussion of Feuerbach see Chapter 4.

PART 2

Learning from
My Mentors

CHAPTER 3

Friedrich Schleiermacher

God Is Experienced

In the summer of 1799 a book entitled *On Religion: Speeches to its Cultured Despisers* was published anonymously in Berlin. As the title implies, it was already becoming obvious that a number of educated people were distancing themselves from traditional Christianity. The book, which attempted to address that situation, immediately became a best-seller, and the identity of the author was soon revealed. He was a young clergyman and hospital chaplain named Friedrich Schleiermacher.

Today Schleiermacher (1768–1834) is hardly known outside academic circles even though this book launched him into an academic career of great distinction. He was not only the first Dean of the Theological Faculty of the University of Berlin, which he helped to found, but a pioneer in the modern study of religions, and arguably the first modern theologian. And although he later came under considerable criticism, he dominated Protestant thought throughout the nineteenth century. At his death the celebrated church historian Neander said, "We have lost a man from whom will be dated henceforth a new era in the history of Theology". In 1913 W. B. Selbie, an Oxford theologian, wrote of him, "He was the originator of a new method

---

This lecture was first delivered under the auspices of St Andrew's Trust for the Study of Religion and Society, Wellington, New Zealand, and published by it as Chapter 1 of *Religious Trailblazers*, 1992.

and the embodiment of a new spirit. . . . He first applied to the study of Christian Theology the modern scientific spirit and methods".

What was the new theological method that Schleiermacher originated? He recognized that assured knowledge of God could no longer be gained through human reason or the dogmatic teaching of the church long accepted as divine revelation. He therefore turned from these traditional and external sources to his own inner experience. In doing so—we can now say with the gift of hindsight—he was unwittingly returning to the matrix of all religious experience and thought.

Schleiermacher's break with tradition is best illustrated by a little composition that was not intended as a serious theological work, but in which some scholars find all the essentials of his new theological method. In December 1804 he went home after a flute concert and, in a mood of sudden inspiration, wrote what he called *Christmas Eve: A Dialogue on the Celebration of Christmas.* He intended to publish it privately and give it to his friends as a Christmas present.

In this charming familiar essay he describes a homely fireside scene at which a gathering of friends (five women and four men) discuss what the celebration of Christmas means to each of them. This format for a religious discussion had been effectively used twenty-five years earlier by the philosopher David Hume, who in turn had borrowed it from Plato. (Schleiermacher was very familiar with the *Dialogues of Plato*, his German translation of which is still in use today).

But the friendly group chosen by Schleiermacher were not academic philosophers discussing abstract and arcane topics; they were ordinary people expressing how they thought about their own religious experience. Moreover, at a time when theology and even group discussion was still regarded as a male preserve, here we find it is the women who initiate the discussion. They interpret the Nativity scene in the light of their feelings and experience. Some are mothers, one is a prospective mother. Others draw from their childhood days. One claims, for example, that she regards Mary as a representation of every mother, who sees her own child as an eternal divine child in whom she looks for the first stirrings of the higher spirit. "Mary has shown us", says another, "what that childlike sense is, without which one cannot enter the Kingdom of God".

When the men subsequently take over the conversation, it moves to a more philosophical and, at times, impersonal level. Leonard, for example, is even said by his friends to be the 'thinking, reflective, dialectical, over-intellectual man'. He is aware that historical study of the Bible is already introducing uncertainty as to how much is really known about the historical Jesus. For him the story of Christ's birth at Bethlehem is at best only a legend, and he doubts whether the organized church reflects the intention of Jesus.

Ernst counters this scepticism by starting from the religious feeling that the celebration of Christmas generates. He sees Christmas as a universal festival of joy. Its continuing significance arises from what Christians have found to be vital in their own Christian experience, and does not depend on whether the biblical story of the birth and life of Jesus is historically true.

In contrast to both, Edward the host is more speculative and mystical. He observes that the Fourth Gospel makes no mention at all of Jesus' birth; instead it asserts that the Word that was with God and *was* God became flesh. The significance of Christmas for Edward is that "what we celebrate is nothing other than ourselves as whole beings—that is, our human nature, or whatever else you want to call it, viewed and known from the perspective of the divine. . . . What else is humankind than the very spirit of earth, or life's coming to know itself in its eternal being and in its ever changing process of becoming?" (In 1803, and before the idea of evolution had spread, this was surely a most radical thought!)

Edward then elaborates his own understanding of humankind's fallen condition, from which it is restored to wholeness by fellowship within the church. Since Christ is the foundation of the church then "each one of us beholds in the birth of Christ his own higher birth whereby nothing lives in him but devotion and love; and in him too the eternal Son of God appears".

Joseph, who arrives later in the evening, is a simple, naive and pious Christian who is rather shocked to find the men arguing almost heatedly on such an occasion. He reacts strongly to the coldly rationalist approach of Leonard and rejects all historical and scholarly criticism as irrelevant. For him Christmas takes him into a "better world where pain and grief no longer have any meaning" and as a result he feels like a child born anew. He tries to restore some cheerful harmony to the evening and the party ends with singing. It was probably quite deliberate on Schleiermacher's part to associate harmonious fellowship with the women and intellectual discord with the men, just as it was to end not with statements of belief, but with the feelings engendered in a fellowship celebrating their common bonds.

One suspects that Schleiermacher's own position is represented not so much by any particular character as by their complex interaction. He could identify with the naively pious Joseph, the mystical Edward, the rationalist Leonard, and with the deep feelings of both Ernst and the women. Furthermore, he appears to have believed that women have a unique advantage over men because of their intuitive ability to penetrate to the heart of an issue; indeed, he once confessed he would rather have been born a woman.

The most important thing to note is that these people all spoke out of their own experience. They did not appeal to the authority of the Bible, but interpreted Christmas (here symbolic of the whole Christian message) just as they experienced it. The pioneering significance of Schleiermacher is that just when the traditional foundations for Christian theology were disintegrating, he shifted attention from the Bible and traditional dogma to internal personal experience. This involved a switch of focus from the objective to the subjective, a change involving a number of dangers that his later critics were quick to point out.

Today we can readily see that Schleiermacher did not allow sufficiently for the uniqueness of personal experiences that were by no means universal. Not only had he been born into the devout home of a Protestant minister and a society deeply permeated by Protestant devotion, but his secondary schooling took place in the intensely religious atmosphere of the Moravian community that he later spoke of as his spiritual womb. This was the supportive experience that stood him in good stead when in late adolescence he encountered the full impact of the coldly intellectual world outside, and when, as he said, he "began to sift the faith of his fathers and to cleanse thought and feeling from the rubbish of antiquity". It was the same inner experience that sustained him when "the God and immortality of my childhood vanished from my doubting eyes".

Schleiermacher assumed that what had been so real and gripping for him was common to all Christians and potentially available to all humans. He spoke of it as the "feeling of absolute dependence", by which he meant something much more than a childlike dependence. It was rather the feeling of being a small part of a greater whole. That is why he also called it 'God-consciousness', explaining it thus: "Along with the absolute dependence which characterizes not only humankind but all temporal existence, there is given to humankind also the immediate self-consciousness of it, which becomes a consciousness of God". This universally available God-consciousness rather than revealed Dogma was the starting-point and basis for Schleiermacher's theology. He believed God-consciousness to be *sui generis* and irreducible to anything else. Therefore it can no more be adequately described in words than sight can be explained to a person born blind. But just as all normal beings

are born with sight, so Schleiermacher believed that all normal
humans have some experience of God-consciousness.

Schleiermacher therefore concluded that the primary data
for theological reflection are not the inherited dogmas of divine
revelation nor the conclusions of rational argument, but the
individual's inner religious experience. This enabled him to acknowledge the inadequacy of all religious concepts and language
and to see that these are always secondary to religious experience. He said, "The usual conception of God as one single being
outside of the world and behind the world is not the beginning
and the end of religion. It is only one manner of expressing God,
seldom entirely pure and always inadequate. . . . The true nature
of religion is neither this idea nor any other, but the immediate
consciousness of the Deity as *He is found in ourselves and in the
world*" (italics mine). He thus rescued what he took to be true
religion from enslavement to unchangeable doctrines. "God and
immortality are ideas", he said, "and as ideas they can have no
greater value than ideas generally".

In spite of his new freedom to criticize traditional concepts
and dogmas, it is apparent that Schleiermacher had been so
conditioned by his Christian upbringing that the theology he
constructed on the rediscovered foundation of inner experience
contained many affirmations that today look remarkably orthodox. This appearance of orthodoxy stood him in good stead, for
he did not suffer the fate of being condemned or ostracised in his
own day as were Aquinas, Luther, and later Feuerbach in theirs.
He was always seen to be within the bounds of Christian orthodoxy, even though considered theologically suspect because of
pantheistic tendencies and judged defective in his understanding
of sin and the person of Jesus Christ. He was very much loved
by those who knew him. Besides attracting many students to his
lectures he also preached practically every Sunday of his life, and
nearly all of Berlin turned out to honour him at his funeral. All

this tends to disguise the radical nature of the changes in religious thought he was pioneering.

Yet within his otherwise orthodox affirmations of Christian faith were elements that might shock conventional Christians even today. For example, what Schleiermacher regarded as the uniqueness of Jesus Christ he described as "the constant power of His God-consciousness". He thought Jesus was as completely human as ourselves; the only difference being that the God-consciousness we experience only partially was fully developed in him. For Schleiermacher the redeeming role of Jesus Christ was in no way dependent on his supposed Virgin Birth, Resurrection and Ascension. He also believed on the evidence of the Gospels that the disciples had come to recognise Jesus as the Christ without reference to these doctrines, and regarded that of the Virgin Birth to be quite superfluous to Christian faith. Whether one accepted the teachings of the Resurrection and the Ascension, depended on the way one understood and interpreted the Bible. "Belief in these facts is no element in the original faith in Christ", he wrote, "and all that can be required of any Protestant Christian is that he shall believe them in so far as they seem to him to be adequately attested". He regarded these not as matters of faith at all, but as issues to be decided by the biblical scholar, the historian and the scientist.

Most surprising of all, perhaps, was Schleiermacher's stand on personal immortality. Even today, traditional Christians are likely to be offended by what he said in *On Religion*: "The immortality that most men imagine and their longing for it seems to me irreligious, nay quite opposed to the spirit of piety. . . . The goal and the character of the religious life is not the immortality desired and believed in by many. . . . It is the immortality we can now have in this temporal life. . . . In the midst of finitude to be one with the Infinite and in every moment to be eternal is the immortality of religion". In his magnum opus, *The Christian*

Faith, Schleiermacher was more cautious and formal; yet even there he warns that the paragraphs he devoted to the Last Things "cannot have ascribed to them at all the same value as the previous doctrines", and he goes so far as to assert, "The question as to the conditions of existence after death is a purely cosmological question". In other words, it is not so much a religious issue as one to be answered on scientific grounds.

As we have just noted, in *The Christian Faith* Schleiermacher appears more orthodox than in his earlier book *On Religion*. It is in the latter that we see more clearly Schleiermacher's originality. Consequently this was the book that went through three editions in his lifetime and continued to be reprinted and translated thereafter. As late as 1926 it was being described as "one of the classical works of . . . theological literature". Schleiermacher explained in a foreword to the third edition that while the book had been written to respond to the attacks of the 'cultured despisers' of religion, he later found he had to defend himself against the religious fanatics who wanted to return to pre-Enlightenment orthodoxy and to extinguish the whole development he had pioneered.

Let us now summarize the main points of that development and see how it led to a much more open religious situation than even he foresaw. First, he made personal religious experience the starting-point for theological reflection by citing as primary data his own experience, spiritual encounters that could not be taken away from him. Thus he was like the blind man in John 9, who when challenged by the Pharisees to denounce Jesus as a sinner, replied, "Whether he is a sinner I do not know; one thing I do know, that though I was blind, now I see".

In the course of attempting to commend Christianity to its 'cultured despisers', Schleiermacher rediscovered in personal human experience the origin not only of Christianity in particular but of all religion in general. The traditional order had long been, and for traditional Christians still is, 'believe the doctrine and the experience of salvation will follow'. This he reversed to read, 'Out of Christian experience emerges the doctrine; this is how it occurred in primitive Christianity, and this is how it must continue today'. This enabled him to recognize that doctrines, affirmations, creeds, and indeed the whole theological enterprise are secondary to the living experience and hence always relative to time, place and person. Because religious experience is always personal, it necessarily differs from person to person and certainly from age to age. None of the authoritative verbal expressions of faith can ever be treated as final and absolute or regarded as mandatory for others to accept. He said that one should not expect creedal uniformity, observing, "As nothing is more irreligious than to demand general uniformity in mankind, so nothing is more unchristian than to seek uniformity in religion".

Of particular importance in Schleiermacher's emphasis on individual sensibility is the way he drew attention to the whole range of human experience, which includes feelings and motivations as well as rational thinking. It was especially in the area of feeling that he found the cold rationalism of the Enlightenment to be sadly lacking; this absence explained why the origin and true nature of religion had been misunderstood and lost sight of. Premodern Christianity, particularly Protestantism, had often become so intellectual and didactic that it paved the way to an arid rationalism. Schleiermacher was aided in rediscovering the emotive aspect of religious experience by his life among the Moravians and his association with the Romantic poets. Today, in the light of depth psychology and our better understanding of the human condition, we can more fully appreciate Schleiermacher's emphasis on the noncognitive aspects of religious experience: for not only do our thoughts help to shape our feelings, but even more important is the fact that our feelings often determine what we think.

Several important things follow from Schleiermacher's switch of attention from the inherited tradition to personal experience.

First, it enables a person to relate his/her experience to the current knowledge and science of the time. The authoritative formulations of doctrine often contained ideas and beliefs about the world that had become obsolete for later generations, and this new freedom was extremely important at a time when the modern scientific enterprise was about to produce a knowledge explosion. Schleiermacher's theological method disentangled religious experience from questions of science and history—a separation earlier pointed out in his distinction between empirical truth and doctrinal claims.

Further, it follows that once creeds, confessions, and traditional dogmas are reduced to secondary status and no longer treated as absolute, the differences among the various denominations of the church have also become of secondary importance. In Schleiermacher we see some of the first signs of the Christian ecumenical movement that was to become prominent in the twentieth century. Although reared in Calvinism, Schleiermacher had no interest in perpetuating denominational divisions; his primary concern was not Calvinist experience, but *religious* experience. Of course for him personally this meant *Christian* experience. He acknowledged that formidable differences between Catholics and Protestants remained, due in part to their common disposition to be exclusive, as well as to ignore and remain inexcusably ignorant of each other. He thought the opposition had already peaked and the tide was beginning to turn. In any case, despite his strong defence of Protestantism he was able to say that the idea of Christianity had found characteristic expression in each and "only by conjoining both, can the historical phenomenon of Christianity correspond to the idea of Christianity".

Moreover because Schleiermacher was concerned with religious experience of the most basic kind, his ecumenical tendencies were not confined to Christendom. The German title of his magnum opus was not *The Christian Faith* but *Glaubenslehre*, which means 'The Doctrine of Faith'. By focusing on the inner experience of faith or God-consciousness, and not specifically on God (as the term 'theology' implies) he was pointing to an experience that is at least potentially universal in humankind. Moreover, Schleiermacher was fully aware that he was thus acknowledging that positive connections exist between Christianity and other religions. "All forms of religion, even the most imperfect, are the same in kind", he said. Of course this strongly repudiated the traditional assertion that Christianity alone is God's truth and all other religions represent various forms of idolatry and superstition. Schleiermacher took a more positive view. Although convinced that Christianity was the highest form of religion, he believed that all religions arose from the basic human capacity for 'God-consciousness' and simply manifest different stages of development. In this respect he regarded the monotheistic religions, which include Judaism and Islam, as constituting the highest level.

Even that view may seem parochial and chauvinistic today, but it was most unusual, and indeed provocative, for a Christian theologian in the early nineteenth century to be as liberal as he was. After all, this was the century in which Protestant missionaries were to take the 'light of the Gospel' to India, Africa and China, to people who were judged to be living in 'heathen darkness'. It was several generations before Christians from the West would recognize positive values in the religions of Asia, and, when they did, it was partly due to the influence of Schleiermacher that they were able to discern common elements in the experiences of Christians, Hindus and Buddhists.

Among the best examples of this development is that of Rudolf Otto (1869–1937), who as Professor of Systematic Theology at Breslau and Marburg, became one of the chief exponents of the modern study of religion variously known as comparative religion, history of religion, or simply religious studies. In his epoch-making book *The Idea of the Holy* (1923)

Otto isolated what he called 'the sense of the numinous'. He believed this to be a universal human experience, the common element in all religions, and the source of all religion. Otto openly acknowledged his debt to Schleiermacher and credited him with the modern rediscovery of the numinous. He wrote, "Without falling back again into the trammels of a primitive supernaturalism he prepared the way to a rediscovery not only of religion but of Christian religion and to a new interpretation of Christian religion, which was better and more modern than the old orthodox or rationalistic theology could give".

The new interpretation of Christianity for which Schleiermacher prepared the way is often known as Protestant liberalism. But Schleiermacher opened up a Pandora's box from which eventually issued a great deal that he did not foresee. As Paul Tillich rightly pointed out a century later, as soon as one dispenses with external divine authorities and makes personal God-consciousness one's starting point, then miracles are not the only things to crumble: "The idea of an existing person called 'God' and the idea of continuation of life after the death of a conscious person, or the idea of immortality, collapse as well". So Karl Barth, a century later, complained that Schleiermacher's new theological method had heralded the end of Christian doctrine as it had been known in the past. "The question as to how it was that Schleiermacher himself was not alarmed by this result, and how he could think . . . that he was not destroying Reformation theology, . . . how he failed to notice that his result challenged the decisive premise of all Christian theology . . . —this question presents us with a mystery which cannot be solved".

Of course Schleiermacher had no intention of destroying Reformation theology or of undermining Christianity itself. Because he did not foresee all that his new method would lead to, he did not fully appreciate just how radical a change he was instrumental in bringing. Karl Barth strongly rejected his method, and to counteract its effects initiated what has been called neo-orthodoxy.

But many others, both before and after Karl Barth, have continued in the path opened up by Schleiermacher. They include such great figures as Rudolf Otto, Rudolf Bultmann and Paul Tillich, as well as my own teacher John Dickie, who was largely responsible for liberalizing Christian thought in the Presbyterian Church of New Zealand during the first half of the twentieth century. The influence of Schleiermacher is clearly recognizable in Dickie's definition of theology as "religious conviction endeavouring to think itself out, and to relate itself to all other knowledge and opinion". This means that religious thought must always be relevant to and consistent with the kind of world in which one lives.

Dickie further insisted that "a living theology is always the self-expression of vital religious faith", thereby implying that to base one's beliefs solely on traditional doctrine is to embrace a secondhand faith. At its very worst this means mouthing a creed composed by others and denying one's integrity—in short, becoming a ventriloquist's dummy.

More recently a number of women theologians have acknowledged their debt to Schleiermacher. For example, Daphne Hampson writes, "I find the thought of Friedrich Schleiermacher, sometimes designated the founder of modern theology, to be an inspiration. Schleiermacher opened up the possibility of conceiving that it is through our knowing of ourselves that we come to a perception of God. God is not to be known apart from ourselves, though God is more than are we".

The greatness of Schleiermacher is that he was among the first to realise that one could no longer speak convincingly to modern intelligent people, 'cultured despisers of religion', by simply expounding the traditional Christian dogmas and seeking support in the traditional authorities. In the modern cultural climate it has become necessary both to allow and to challenge people to speak out of their own experience. It is true that such an approach may lead to considerable religious diversity, including even potentially dangerous aberrations. But such is the nature of the modern world that came to birth during the Enlightenment: people are now free to think for themselves and to make their own judgments about what is true. Truth must rest on its inherent capacity to convince and not on the authority of the priest, the Bible, the scholar or even the scientist.

This does not mean that everything we experience is genuinely religious or that one form of experience is just as good as another. What it does mean is that all our theology and reflection on ultimate issues should start with our own experience, which we should subject to critical scrutiny, employing such light as we can borrow from others and also glean from the past.

This essentially new situation in which modern humankind finds itself, in contrast with that of our premodern forebears, has been called 'mankind's coming of age'. Schleiermacher recognized this to be the situation, and both consciously and unconsciously pioneered a theological method to suit it. Whether we know his name or not, we are all in his debt. He who could imagine a theological discourse on Christianity initiated by women would surely have rejoiced at the recent entry of women into the arena of academic theology. Schleiermacher has opened the door for all of us, women and men, nonspecialists as well as academics, to participate in the theological enterprise and to think through for ourselves, in the presence and with the encouragement of others, the significance of those experiences that we personally have found most meaningful, most holy, and of ultimate concern.

CHAPTER 4

Ludwig Feuerbach

God Is Humanity Projected

In 1824 Ludwig Feuerbach, a young theological student at Heidelberg, went up to Berlin to study under the already famous theologian Friedrich Schleiermacher. But after only a year he transferred to philosophy, having come under the spell of the equally famous Friedrich Georg Hegel (1770–1831). Hegel dominated the philosophical world of the nineteenth century in much the same way as Schleiermacher dominated Protestant theology. Though they were colleagues at the same university they shared little in matters of religion. Hegel once remarked that if true religion consisted in a feeling of absolute dependence, as Schleiermacher said it did, then "the dog would be the best Christian".

Like Schleiermacher, Hegel also began his studies with theology, and all of his early writings were theological. But he soon became disillusioned with Christian orthodoxy and tried to resolve the growing conflict between Christianity and modern culture by a method very different from that of Schleiermacher, and in the process constructed a highly ambitious philosophical system. Along the way he offered a number of fascinating new insights into the most profitable way of understanding some of the central stories of the Bible, many of which were later taken

This lecture was first delivered under the auspices of St Andrew's Trust for the Study of Religion and Society, Wellington, New Zealand, and published by it as Chapter 2 of *Religious Trailblazers*, 1992.

up by others. For example, he was the first to treat the story of Adam's Fall and the account of Jesus' Resurrection as myths rather than as historical events. He said they were parables—symbolic stories that had deep philosophical meaning.

Hegel interpreted the Garden of Eden story in a much more positive way than Christian tradition had done. Far from representing humankind's fall from grace in a far distant past, he took it to portray an evolutionary transformation from animallike innocence—the lack of awareness of good and evil—to human self-consciousness, in which we suffer from that very awareness. "The Fall is the myth of the human condition", he said; "it symbolizes the very transition by which we develop from an animal into a human state".

Similarly he was among the first of modern thinkers to see that the significance of the narratives of the resurrection of Jesus lay outside the realm of history. "To consider the resurrection of Jesus as an event is to adopt the outlook of the historian and this has nothing to do with religion", he said. "As a human individual Jesus lived, died on the cross and was buried". "Resurrection is something which essentially belongs to faith", he said, and saw it as a symbolic description of the way Christ's spirit came to life in the disciples, and subsequently in the church down through the generations. His categorization of some biblical material as myth rather than history was soon to be more thoroughly developed by his young disciple David Strauss (1808–74), whose book *The Life of Jesus Critically Examined* in 1835 has been judged "a turning point in the history of the Christian faith". The storm of indignation it aroused led to Strauss being dismissed from his university post.

Before this, however, Hegel had already been developing his radical thinking in other directions. He believed the traditional concept of God had become obsolete, being far too limited a notion to suit the greatly expanded view of the universe then opening up. "God is no longer to be conceived as a person or as a being above and beyond this world", he said. Hegel treated God as the name of the one and only true reality, besides which no other reality can claim independent existence. We humans, he believed, participate in the reality of God, and our human self-consciousness is all part and parcel of the self-consciousness of God. "The idea a man has of God corresponds with that which he has of himself. . . . When a man knows truly about God, he knows truly about himself also".

These were only a few of the seed-thoughts that were sown in the mind of the young Feuerbach. But though along with Strauss and Karl Marx Feuerbach is usually remembered as one of the 'young Hegelians', he is a particularly good example of the radical extremes to which Schleiermacher's new method could lead. Feuerbach always retained a positive attitude towards religion (which Marx of course did not) and he made Schleiermacher's starting point the basis of what he called 'the new philosophy' that he outlined in his *Principles of the Philosophy of the Future*: "The new philosophy rests on the truth of love and feeling. . . . The new philosophy itself is basically nothing other than the essence of feeling elevated to consciousness; it only affirms in reason and with reason what every man—the real man—professes in his heart. It is the heart made into mind. . . . The new philosophy . . . recognizes the truth of sensation with joy and consciousness; it is the open-hearted and sensuous philosophy". In those words one can immediately detect the influence of Schleiermacher. Indeed, it was Schleiermacher's view concerning human feelings and emotions as the origin and confirmation of religion that enabled Feuerbach to look at Hegel's philosophical system critically—and quite literally to turn Hegel upside down.

The act of turning Hegel on his head has often been attributed to Marx, but it was actually Feuerbach who achieved this remarkable feat. To understand what that means, we need to look briefly at Hegel's philosophical system. It belongs to the stream of philosophy known as idealism and is its chief modern example. By idealism is meant the conviction that the eternal stuff of reality is not physical matter but ideas, abstract truths, thought, mind. For this basic reality Hegel used the German word *Geist* which can be translated as both mind and spirit. Thus for Hegel 'God' and 'Geist' are synonymous; as mentioned above, Hegel treated 'God' as the name of the only true reality.

But how, then, did the physical universe come into existence? As Hegel saw it, the physical world and all living creatures, including ourselves, are the creation of Geist; they are not a creation out of nothing but an emanation from Geist itself and that is why we humans continue to manifest and participate in the reality of Geist. Our minds are, as it were, part of the mind of God. Our bodies are temporal and dispensable; but through our minds we have a share in eternity.

The influence of both Hegel and Schleiermacher began to work in the young Feuerbach, who in 1839 had a sudden flash of insight resembling a kind of religious conversion. He became convinced that Hegel's grasp of truth was upside down. Hegel had "made spirit the parent of matter" but the real truth is that "matter was the parent of spirit". Hegel conceived physical matter as emanating from mind; Feuerbach was convinced that mind emanated from physical matter in the shape of human organisms. Hegel began with spirit and had to explain the existence of physical matter; Feuerbach started from physical matter and explained how it gave rise to human consciousness, ideas, culture and all that is involved in human spirituality. Hegel expounded an idealist philosophy; Feuerbach its materialist inversion.

While materialist philosophy can be variously understood, few will deny that it is the philosophical basis of modern science and represents the prevailing view in today's world. Even in the human sphere, where we still use terms that refer to such abstract or nonphysical realities as soul, mind, art, justice, goodness, and so on, we are quick to trace these categories back to their human sources. In short, we have come increasingly to recognize that humans are beings whose very existence arises from and depends on their physical bodies. Feuerbach once tried to drive this home with the epigram "Man is what he eats," which in German employs a clever pun: "*Der Mensch ist was er isst*".

But though Feuerbach was a materialist in his philosophy it does not mean that he treated lightly the spiritual dimension of human existence. Far from it! He saw in human culture and specifically in religion the essential difference between humans and animals. He always contended that his writings had only one theme, which was nothing less than religion and theology and all that is connected with them.

Yet that was not the way religious people of the day saw him. His very first publication landed him in deep trouble at the age of 26. It was entitled *Thoughts on Death and Immortality*—an essay of which he later remarked that it already contained the outline of his whole philosophy. In it he said, "Man is not only a spiritual being, he is also an earthly being, inseparable from the earth". This meant that our personal destiny is confined to our existence on this side of death and that there can be no conscious existence for us on the other. This publication caused such an uproar that he was dismissed from his academic post and compelled to spend the rest of his life as a private scholar.

In 1841, at the age of 37, he completed his most celebrated work *The Essence of Christianity*. It became the most talked about book of the decade, and in 1854 was translated into English by George Eliot. But even then his fame in Germany was declining. In the eyes of the theologians he was too humanistic and atheistic; in the eyes of Hegelian socialists like Karl Marx, he remained too religious. Yet he had a considerable impact on such important later figures as Nietzsche, Troeltsch, Freud, Heidegger, Sartre, and perhaps most important of all, as we shall later see, the Jewish philosopher Martin Buber. Even Karl Barth, who was naturally very critical of Feuerbach's basic position, conceded that "No philosopher of his time penetrated the contemporary theological situation as effectually as he, and few spoke with such pertinence".

What then did he say? His magnum opus is divided into two parts. In the second part he argued that traditional theology had offered a false exposition of Christianity, whereas the first and longer part presented an exposition of what he called the true or humanly based understanding of Christianity. In the very first chapter he reflected the influence of Schleiermacher: "where feeling is held to be the subjective essence of religion, then the external facts of religion already begin to lose their objective value".

Feuerbach judged the philosophical system of Hegel to be "the last magnificent attempt to restore Christianity", but in his view this had been achieved only by conceiving God to be "nothing other than the essence of thought". Hegel had turned thought into a divine and absolute being. Yet what is thought, asked Feuerbach, but the creation of the human mind? Hegel's God, therefore, is a projection on to the cosmic backdrop of something emanating from the human mind. Hegel's God was the creation of Hegel himself, and what is true of Hegel's God is true of God generally. In other words, Feuerbach maintained, 'God' is an idea in the human mind, a concept first created by our human ancestors in the distant cultural past and then transmitted in culture from generation to generation.

In turning Hegel upside down (or as Feuerbach insisted, "turning him the right way up"), Feuerbach was also reversing traditional Christianity's understanding of God. It had always been taught that God had made humans in his own image; Feuerbach asserted that we humans have made 'God' in *our* own image. "The personality of God is nothing else than the projection of the personhood we find in humankind". And for support he quoted from the great philosopher Kant who had said, "Fundamentally we cannot conceive God otherwise than by attributing to him without limit all the real qualities we find in ourselves". Feuerbach even claimed that St Anselm, Archbishop of Canterbury in the eleventh century, had unwittingly conceded this point in his famous proof of the existence of God, where he defined God as the name of "that than which nothing greater can be conceived". That is, said Feuerbach, "God is the highest idea you can have, the supreme effort of your understanding, the highest power of your thinking".

This reversal of the relationship between God and human-kind immediately rendered Feuerbach an atheist in the eyes of traditionalists, and on that basis he came to be rejected by both the church and the academic community. Feuerbach was in full accord with atheists that, if by 'God' we mean an "abstract dis-embodied being distinct from nature and man, who decides the fate of the world and of mankind as he pleases", then there is no God. But he sought to distinguish himself very clearly from atheists who saw no further than that. The rejection of that false view of God was only half of the proper task of theology, and belonged in the same category as the rejection of idolatry. Much more important for Feuerbach was the difficult task of under-standing why the concept of God had been created in the first place and of appreciating what was really true about this word.

In the first part of his seminal book Feuerbach went to great lengths to explain what he found to be true within the Christian tradition, beginning with the truth expressed in the concept of God. This concept was not to be dismissed, as it was by the atheist; rather the idea of God was to be truly valued for what it was. The Russian novelist Dostoyevski was probably reflect-ing the influence of Feuerbach when, in his novel *The Brothers Karamazov* (1880), he put these words into the mouth of Ivan: "What is strange, what is marvellous, is not whether God really exists; the marvel is that such an idea, the idea of the necessity of God, could have entered the head of such a savage and vicious beast as man; so holy it is, so moving, so wise, and such a great honour it does to man".

For Feuerbach, the reason why the word 'God' survived the decline of the primitive mythology in which it had originated is that monotheism gradually came to portray symbolically all that humans have come to value most highly, all the goals they have aspired to, all the skills of power and knowledge they have most admired.

This process has taken place quite unconsciously, of course; our ancestors were quite unaware that they were projecting their own values in this way. Yet the fact is confirmed by traditional theology's preoccupation with the *attributes* of God (i.e. the values of love, justice, omniscience, etc.) rather than the *being* of God (which was assumed to be beyond human understanding anyway).

This being the case, Feuerbach asserted, the concept of God should not be dismissed as having no meaning. It has a very important meaning, for it refers in symbolic language to the highest dimension of human existence, our spirituality. Religion and religious terms, along with art, philosophy and science, manifest this awe-inspiring potential to be found in the human condition. When we talk about God we are using symbolic terms to explore the full potential of the human condition. "Consciousness of God is human self-consciousness, knowledge of God is self-knowledge. By his/her God you know the person and by the person his/her God: the two are identical. Whatever is God to a person, that is his/her heart and soul". Thus the study of God turns out to be the study of humankind, and the fundamental truth of theology is that it is an exercise in human self-understanding.

So far so good, Feuerbach implied. If humans had been aware of what they were actually doing in creating their religious language and accompanying rituals it would have proved an entirely healthy undertaking. We humans can benefit greatly from the symbols we create. But the evolution of monotheism ran into trouble because religious language and concepts came to be taken not symbolically, but quite literally. Terms and images that were creations of the human imagination took on an objective reality, and God came to be understood as a personal being—unseen and external to ourselves, but just as objectively real. When that happened, a great gulf opened up between humans and the symbolic concept they had created and projected into the heavens. All that humans admired, valued and aspired came to be embodied in God and they themselves were left with all that they hated about themselves—negative qualities that in later times were projected onto the figure of Satan. Thus the more powerful they conceived God to be, the frailer they saw themselves to be; the holier God became, the more sinful they felt. People envisioned an inverse relation between God's infinitude and perfection and the finite, sinful nature of humankind. It is no accident that Christian teaching and preaching consistently contrasted God's transcendent goodness with the incorrigible wickedness of all humankind. "The concept of the morally perfect being", said Feuerbach, "has the effect of throwing me into disunion with myself; for while it proclaims to me what I ought to be, it also tells me to my face, without any flattery, what I am not".

Feuerbach fully conceded that when traditional Christianity described the human condition as suffering from alienation, it was defining something very real. It was a condition from which humans needed to be delivered. But the alienation had to be understood for what it was and not interpreted as something it was not. Humans have suffered alienation, he argued, because monotheism has caused them to experience a division between the higher self that they have projected into heaven in the form of a personal God and the lower self that remains, causing them to feel unworthy. Therefore, when Christianity preaches reconciliation between God and humankind, it is really proclaiming a restoration of humanity to a state of wholeness and the end of a divided human consciousness.

At this point in his exposition Feuerbach achieved a brilliant tour de force when he pressed home his case by a revolutionary new interpretation of the central Christian doctrine of the incarnation of God in the person of Jesus Christ. To appreciate how Feuerbach achieved this, we need to remember that Strauss had already distinguished clearly between the historical figure of Jesus and the godlike figure of Christ into which the human Jesus had been transformed by the devout imagination of the faithful. Much as Strauss drew this distinction by separating history from myth, Feuerbach distinguished between what he called 'historical facts' and 'religious facts'. The resurrection of Jesus to become the Christ was judged by Feuerbach to be a religious fact; and needless to say, he deemed it a great misunderstanding "to attempt to trace religious facts, that exist only in faith, back to historical facts".

For Feuerbach the doctrine of the incarnation was a symbolic way of explaining how humans had recovered spiritual wholeness by having their divided selves reconciled: God, their highest values, had become enfleshed in them. The reason why it was even feasible that God could assume human flesh is that God originated as a projection of human qualities. For Feuerbach, the doctrine of the incarnation meant that 'God' henceforth would dwell within the human condition where he belonged, leaving the throne of heaven empty. Here one might recall the statement in Revelation 21:3 that "the dwelling of God is with men". Hegel before him had already interpreted the death of Jesus the God-man on the cross as symbolizing the 'death of God'; Feuerbach followed his lead by understanding the crucifixion of Jesus to symbolize the end of theism.

As Feuerbach saw it, it was the supremacy of love that led to the doctrine of the incarnation. He judged love to be the highest of the virtues embodied in the concept of God, so exalted, in fact, that the New Testament could simply say, "God is love". Consequently, and symbolically speaking, it was love that led 'God' to abandon his heavenly throne, empty himself of his otherworldliness, and dwell henceforth within the human condition. This was the real meaning of the incarnation, Feuerbach asserted, and it presented humans with a challenge: Is it 'God' who saves us or is it love? Feuerbach affirmed that it is "Love: for God as God has not saved us but Love, which transcends the difference between the divine and human personality. As God has renounced himself out of love, so we, out of love, should renounce God: for if we do not sacrifice God to love, we sacrifice love to God, and we have . . . the God of religious fanaticism".

No doubt this strikingly insightful observation explains why some of the most intense monotheists, both Christian and Muslim, have also been such unloving and cruel persecutors. Even today we readily find confirmation of Feuerbach's analysis, for those who are most convinced that God is an objective being external to them are the most certain that they know exactly what God thinks and desires on any issue. It is tempting to conclude that their certainty concerning the mind of God derives from the unconscious projection of their own convictions onto a hypothetical spiritual being whose authority they can then claim for acting in accordance with their opinions and beliefs.

Feuerbach's attempt to expound the true essence of Christianity did not stop there. Not all that he said is equally interesting or relevant to us today, and some of his observations may even strike us as superficial. But a further aspect of his understanding of Christianity that arose from his interpretation of the doctrine of the Trinity found favour with many. The strict monotheism we find in Judaism and Islam has always emphasized the singularity or Oneness of God that is exemplified in the Jewish Shema—"The LORD our God is One"—and in the Islamic divine name *Al Wahid* (the One). Christians, by contrast, have affirmed God to be the Three in One.

Feuerbach saw in the Holy Trinity a symbol of the essential importance of human community, a theme on which he himself placed great emphasis. When he spoke of human creativity and greatness, he was not referring to the human individual but to humans in community. For him, "the secret of the Trinity is the secret of communal and social life: it is the truth that no be-ing—man, God, or ego—is for itself alone a true, perfect and absolute being". This, thought Feuerbach, was an unconscious acknowledgement that only in communal existence is the true nature of the human condition expressed.

But Feuerbach felt the Christian doctrine of the Trinity had not been adequately formulated. For him the only true 'persons' in the Trinity were the Father and the Son; and all that the Holy Spirit did was to express, again in a symbolical way, the power of love that unites the Father and the Son, and that similarly unites the individual members of a human community. The third per-son of the Trinity, he thought, should undoubtedly have been the Holy Mother, and he deplored the fact that Protestantism had abandoned the concept of the Mother of God, which had been slowly growing in importance in Christian history. So when Feuerbach contended that the concept of God was in reality the projection of the essence of humanity, he intended 'humanity' to mean 'the human community'. "A human for himself is human (in the ordinary sense); human with human—the unity of I and Thou—is God". "The individual person possesses the essence of humanity neither in himself as a moral being, nor in himself as a thinking being. The essence of humanity is contained only in the community and unity of person with person; it is a unity, however, which rests only the reality of the distinction between I and Thou".

It was this point that came to mean so much to Martin Buber and that he made famous in his spiritual classic *I and Thou*, using words he took over from Feuerbach, who had taken the argument further when he said, "the true dialectic is not a monologue of a solitary thinker with himself; it is a dialogue between I and Thou". Buber came to feel that spiritual power exists in the personal relations that draw people together in reciprocity. It led him to emphasize the value of true dialogue and to suggest a fresh understanding of God as the Eternal Thou present in all deep human relationships of the I-Thou variety.

Such proposals and influences show that, while strongly critical of the supernaturalist religion of the past, Feuerbach was nevertheless committed to a religious understanding of life, even though he saw religion as a human creation. He drew a contrast between the religious person and the nonreligious in this way: "The freethinker is liable to the danger of an unregulated life: . . . The religious man has an aim, and, having an aim, he has firm standing-ground. Every man must place before himself a God, i.e. an aim, a purpose. He who has an aim, an aim which is in itself true and essential has *eo ipso* a religion".

After a few years in the academic wilderness, Feuerbach was invited by the student body of Heidelberg to deliver a short course of lectures in 1848. These he entitled *The Essence of Religion,* and he ended with these words, "We must replace the love of God by the love of man as the only true religion . . . the belief in God by the belief in man, i.e. that the fate of humankind depends not on a being outside of it and above it but on humankind itself. . . . My wish is to transform friends of God into friends of man, believers into thinkers, devotees of prayer into devotees of work, candidates for the hereafter into students of this world, Christians who, by their own profession and admission are half-animal, half-angel, into people. Today they are still less than totally acceptable in all religious circles who are whole". To say such things in his day was revolutionary and outrageous. Today they are still less than totally acceptable in all religious circles, but in secular society they have become almost commonplace. The extent to which that is the case is a measure of how Feuerbach, with all his faults, may be judged a religious trailblazer.

CHAPTER 5

Carl Jung

God Is in the Unconscious

The feverish intellectual activity in nineteenth-century Europe was in large measure the legacy of Hegel and Schleiermacher. It is hard to realise today that Schleiermacher was writing before the intense burst in the historical study of the Bible—a scholarly enterprise that showed the Bible to be wholly of human origin, reflective of the ages and cultures in which it was written, and consequently unable to be regarded as the last word on any topic. As a result, Schleiermacher's theological method was well placed to deal with this crisis, and indeed enabled many to come to terms with it.

It is also easy to forget that Feuerbach was writing several decades before the rise of the modern discipline of psychology. He seemed to stumble upon a psychological understanding of religious experience without the prompting and support that he could have found in that discipline. Were he writing today he certainly would have put some things rather differently, and the main thrust of his argument would have proved all the more convincing.

In this chapter we move to another man whose insights have thrown much positive light on the religious character of the human condition and on the important role played by religious

This lecture was first delivered under the auspices of St Andrew's Trust for the Study of Religion and Society, Wellington, New Zealand, and published by it as Chapter 3 of *Religious Trailblazers*, 1992.

symbolism. But unlike Feuerbach, Carl Jung (1875–1961) came after the rise of the science of psychology. He built on the foundation of his onetime colleague and friend, Sigmund Freud (1856–1939), and then proceeded to pioneer the use of this new discipline to provide a fuller and more sympathetic understanding of the phenomenon of religion.

For most people the name of Freud has become almost synonymous with what is known as depth psychology, since he was the modern discoverer of that great area of the human mind referred to as the subconscious. (I say modern discoverer, for it was a strange but very able Swiss scientist called Paracelsus [1493–1541] who first coined the term 'subconscious'.)

The subconscious (or 'unconscious', the term preferred by Jung) is a vast area of human mental or psychic functioning that lurks beneath the surface of consciousness, just as nine-tenths of an iceberg is hidden under the surface of the ocean. The discovery of the subconscious has made possible an entirely different explanation of what had commonly been called religious experiences. Previously, when a person saw visions invisible to others or heard voices inaudible to others, the most obvious explanation was that these were revelations, messages from an external source of a divine or at least supernatural kind. Those to whom such experiences were described faced a dilemma: either a divine visitation of some kind had occurred or the subject was suffering from illusions associated with madness. Most opted for the former—as we see in the cases of St Paul before Damascus, Muhammad at Mt Hira or St Bernadette at Lourdes. Some opted for the latter, as happened in the case of St Joan of Arc. Depth psychology provides a third explanation, one that avoids the dilemma: these experiences are neither illusory nor indications of madness. Indeed, for the persons concerned they are very real and may change the course of their lives. But far from reflecting the action of some external source, they are wholly internal in origin, for they originate in the unconscious before entering into the conscious area of the mind (a term which Jung preferred to call 'psyche').

The common experience of dreaming is itself reasonable proof that much more goes on in the psyche than reaches the level of awareness. When we dream we are largely or totally unconscious; yet while most of what we dream is quickly forgotten, we often recall enough when we awaken to know that we were dreaming. And although we may choose to dismiss dreams as having no relevance to the real life of our waking hours and commonly do, it was Freud's study of dreams that enabled him to demonstrate that the human psyche is more complex than had previously been thought. He spoke of dreams as the royal road into the unconscious.

Freud was interested in people's dreams chiefly for what they revealed about the inner tensions, repressed memories, and sexual drives of his patients. Not only did he see in them no religious significance, but he came to regard all so-called religious experiences as some form of psychic disorder, for since these experiences could now be traced back to the individual human psyche, attributing them to a supernatural or divine source became highly problematic. In his view, therefore, the content of these experiences was illusory, as was the phenomenon of religion itself. He wrote several books to this effect, one of which was entitled *The Future of an Illusion*.

Carl Jung, Freud's longtime collaborator, reached a very different conclusion, and their relationship ended in a sudden and very painful break. The chief reason was that their understanding of the human unconscious had begun to move in opposite directions. Freud was chiefly concerned with developing what he called psychoanalysis, a therapeutic process for healing psychic illness, whereas Jung became increasingly interested in the way the normal human psyche operates. It thus fell to him to draw attention to the outstanding creative capacity of the unconscious.

Jung viewed the unconscious with much the same awe and wonder as that felt by earlier visitors to what were considered the world's holy places. In studying the human unconscious Jung felt he had drawn close to the source of all human creativity. It was the origin of all that had come to distinguish the human species from other life forms. Here was the wellspring of art, poetry, religion and all the other components of culture.

Thus it was that as time went on, Freud and Jung moved to antithetical positions on the nature and value of religion. For Freud religion was a form of social neurosis from which people needed to be delivered for the sake of their own mental health. Jung, on the other hand, concluded that the absence of a genuine religious outlook resulted in many of the neuroses from which people suffered. Towards the end of his life Jung wrote, "Among all my patients over thirty-five there has not been one whose problem in the last resort was not that of finding a religious outlook on life. Everyone of them fell ill because he had lost what the religions of every age have given to their followers, and none has been really healed who did not regain his religious outlook. This has nothing to do with any particular creed or church".

Jung called his new understanding of the human psyche 'analytical psychology' and delineated various ways in which it throws light on religious experience, two of which are particularly worthy of discussion here: First, it helps to explain why the various religious traditions evolved as they did. Second, it shows that even in today's secular world, religious images, motifs, and symbols still play an important role in promoting human spirituality and may even be essential for psychic health and a fully human experience of life. Let us look at these two in turn.

Jung considered all religious traditions to be rooted in the creative power of the human psyche. He never claimed to know just what the psyche is, but he proposed a model based on both clinical evidence and on his extensive study of cultures past and present. An erudite and extremely well-read scholar, he wrote extensively on such diverse topics as Zen Buddhism, the Tibetan Book of the Dead, medieval alchemy, and the ancient Gnostics.

Common elements and themes in this diverse material led to his model of the psyche. What Freud termed the unconscious, Jung labelled the personal unconscious, and defined it as the depository of all our past personal experiences, including the impact of our mother culture. Many of these elements have long since been forgotten or repressed. But our inability to recall them to consciousness must not be taken to mean either their disappearance or their inactivity. Indeed, some of this stored material may induce or shape the dreams we have, and sometimes it can be brought to the surface by hypnosis. Moreover, we tend to be unaware of the role it often plays in our decision-making processes. The discovery of the unconscious has had the unsettling effect of showing us that our conscious self is not quite as much in control of our actions as we commonly assume it to be.

To be sure, Freud agreed with all of that; but Jung went further. On the basis of his research he postulated that beneath the personal unconscious exists an even deeper level of the unconscious that is substantially the same in us all. This he called the collective unconscious. Just as the personal unconscious preserves the deposit of our personal experience, so the collective unconscious contains and transmits from generation to generation the residue of motifs that have evolved during the long cultural history of the human race and that enrich the creative source upon which our ever developing humanity depends.

If Jung's model is a more or less accurate construct, then the psyche of each individual human is a sort of edifice consisting of three stories that differ greatly in age. Our conscious ego is actually younger than our physical age, for it did not begin to define itself until some months or even years after our birth.

Our personal unconscious goes back at least to birth and may even store some prenatal experiences. But our collective unconscious is as old as our species. "The collective unconscious", Jung wrote, "contains the whole spiritual heritage of mankind's evolution born anew in the brain structure of every individual". This would mean that what goes on in our thinking and in our dreaming is being continually shaped, not only by our experiences within the culture into which we are born, but also by the psychic remnants of our species.

What is in the collective unconscious? Jung never suggested that it consists of anything like the memories found in the personal unconscious. Nor is there any way of delving into it as one can to a limited degree probe the personal unconscious by means of dreams and hypnosis. The collective unconscious must remain a postulation, for evidence of its existence can be derived only from a comparative study of all human cultures.

Therefore, Jung proposed, the collective unconscious is comprised not of memories, but propensities that he called archetypes. This word, which means an originating pattern or prototype, was introduced by the first-century Jewish philosopher Philo and some five centuries later taken up by the mystical Christian theologian known as Dionysius the Areopagite. In Jungian theory archetypes are to the psyche what drives or instincts are to the physical body. They form the embryonic structure of the psyche and provide the patterns for ordering and shaping the psychic material absorbed into the personal unconscious in the course of experience. For example, even before we learn our mother tongue, our tender psyches are already 'programmed' for speech, whereas those of chimpanzees are not. The concept of 'programming', widely familiar in our computer age, is an apt metaphor for this phenomenon; for the archetypes do for the psyche what a computer programme like Word or Excel does for a computer.

Of course Jung was active long before the advent of the computer, and even before much was known of the genetic codes that determine both our humanity and our individuality within the species. What Jung did was to observe that certain basic themes, motifs, and symbols keep cropping up in all ages and in all cultures, and he attributed the persistence of these items to the archetypes. Just as the information conveyed by the genetic code shapes the developing body and also provides the newly born child with instinctive patterns of behaviour that promote survival, so the archetypes order and shape the experiential material entering the psyche through the stream of consciousness.

Jung thought of the unconscious as operating along these lines: The material deposited in the personal unconscious from conscious experience encounters the archetypes present in the collective unconscious and together they form a whirlpool of activity, some of which reveals itself in our dreams. The over-arching purpose of the archetypes of the collective unconscious is to impose a degree of order on human experience and thus to provide it with meaning. As we know from our dreams, the psyche engages in fast-moving dramas that often have no inner consistency, for the operations of the psyche are not dependent on language or logic. The psyche's original and still common currency is not language, but pictures and symbols that are often picturesque, bizarre and colourful. Some are wholly imaginary and some recapture aspects of conscious experience.

Just as biological evolution, once started, generated in the course of time an unbelievable number of variant and diverse zoological species, so the psyche swarms with psychic products— visual images and figures, dramas, and activities of all sorts. The visual arts are one of the best means of appreciating the creative activity of the psyche, for they express its products graphically for all to see. And psychotherapy is able to make such effective use of both the visual and the dramatic arts because these communicative media preceded language and logic, and thus represent the oldest products of the evolving and ever-creative psyche.

Language itself was a product of the psyche, and began to evolve when the exuberant potential of the collective unconscious led to the discovery of how to use vocal sounds symbolically. The emergence of language opened the door to a whole new sphere of creativity—the telling of stories. This was the intermediate stage between simple communication and the very much later creation of meaningful, abstract thought; indeed, dreaming, daydreaming and primitive storytelling exhibit powerful affinities. The Australian aborigine refers to the time of origins as the 'Dream-time', a particularly apposite phrase for the context in which the earliest stories or myths emerged. 'Myth' is simply the ancient Greek word for a story told by word of mouth. "The primitive mentality did not *invent* myths", said Jung, "it *experienced* them. Myths were original revelations of the preconscious psyche. A tribe's mythology is its living religion and its loss is always a moral catastrophe".

Myths are the means by which the collective human unconscious tries to bring some order into the chaos of our experience, to organize our perception of reality, and to resolve the various tensions we experience in our encounter with the external world. Our dreams are myths in the making, even though most of them never come to be told. The psyche has proved itself to be a veritable myth-making factory.

Therefore, religion may be said to have begun with the telling of stories or myths. All religious traditions depend for their continuing vitality on a cycle of myths. The Christian myths, for example, include the story of Adam and Eve, the fall from innocence, the incarnation of God in human flesh by a virginal birth, the reconciling death of Jesus on the cross, his resurrection and ascension to heaven, his coming again, the Last Judgment. The power of these myths lies not in their historicity but in their symbolism. "It is the role of religious symbols", said Jung, "to give meaning to human life". Those who embrace the Christian faith use these myths symbolically to interpret their own experience in the light of them. The myths provide them with their values and their goals and enable them to live their lives in an ordered, meaningful and spiritually satisfying way. A religious tradition, and the myths which compose it, promote mental wholeness or health and a sense of spiritual fulfilment. That is why Carl Jung described religions as the 'world's great psychotherapeutic symbol-systems'.

According to Jung the archetypes perform two roles. One, as we have just noted, is to supply the motifs that give order to the chaos of experience; the other is to structure the developing psyche itself. Because the stream of consciousness that flows from birth onwards needs a unifying centre to enable the individual to develop a conscious identity, the archetypical Ego arises from the collective unconscious to supply that need. It forms at the centre of consciousness a strong sense of self—the Ego-identity. It is the conscious 'I'.

The Ego acts as a kind of controller, selecting from the wealth of data presented to it those on which it chooses to focus attention. As time goes on and consciousness develops into self-consciousness, the Ego assumes an increasingly responsible role in decision-making. The Ego exercises a mediating function between the signals coming from the outer world and the continuing motivational demands arising from the unconscious.

Being an internal spiritual entity, the Ego can be fragile, vulnerable and easily wounded; hence it needs a protection from the external world. Jung gave the name of Persona to this shield, itself the creation of an archetype. He borrowed the Latin word for the mask worn by ancient actors to identify their roles, ancient theologians having already used it to express the several roles of God in their doctrine of the Trinity. The Persona is the face one chooses to show to the world, and is reflected in one's dress, general appearance and habitual behaviour.

When the Ego is reaching mature self-consciousness, the adequacy of the Persona becomes most important. Part of the trauma of puberty and growth to adulthood results from the struggle to discover the most appropriate Persona. Because of the complexity of modern life and the variety of contexts in which we find ourselves, we tend to develop multiple Personas, to assume slightly different roles in different surroundings. But if these roles vary too much, or if our Persona becomes too alienated from our Ego, we all too soon are seen to be insincere or shallow.

Besides the signals from the external world we have to deal with prehuman and even primal urges that we have inherited from the earliest forms of life. These Jung referred to collectively as the Shadow, observing that this element of the psyche is not so much evil as amoral—or even better, premoral. It is the residue of the prehuman animal psyche that has not yet been adapted to the restraints of culture. The Ego often finds itself struggling against the Shadow, a conflict it does not understand because the Shadow is hidden from consciousness.

One of the most lucid expressions of it is found in the Bible in some well-known words of St Paul (Romans 7:15–20):

> I do not understand my own actions. For I do the very thing I hate. . . . So then it is no longer I (*Ego*) that do it, but sin (*Shadow*) that dwells within me, that is in my flesh (*unconscious*). I can will what is right but I cannot do it. For I do not do the good I want, but the evil I do not want is what I do. Now if I do what I do not want, it is no longer I (*Ego*) that do it, but sin (*Shadow*) that dwells in me.

If the Shadow is ignored or repressed, it may trigger outrageous behaviour. And it is common for a repressed Shadow to be unconsciously projected onto somebody else who displays the urges that we refuse to acknowledge in ourselves. In medieval Christendom the collective Shadow of the human species was projected onto the mythical figure of Satan or the Devil. By blaming him for wicked actions, one was able to disclaim full responsibility for one's actions. Wherever people display exaggerated condemnation of some criminal action or sexual misbehaviour, they are likely to be projecting some aspect of the Shadow that lurks within themselves.

The most important archetype of all for the structuring of the psyche is the archetype of the Self, which is not to be confused with the Ego. Whereas the Ego is the centre of consciousness, the Self is the centre of the whole psyche, including both consciousness and the unconscious. The archetype of the Self has the function of promoting psychic unity by harmonizing the many psychic components and developing the psyche to its mature potential. The process of becoming a mature, whole and harmonious self is what Jung called individuation.

This process, he thought, takes place in two successive periods. In the first half of life, roughly up to the age of forty, the main task of the psyche is to become fully adjusted to the external world. It involves the growth of a firm Ego identity and the establishment of an adequate Persona. In the second half of life the main task of the psyche is to come to terms with one's own inner reality, to acknowledge one's Shadow, and to accept one's limitations—including one's mortality. This growth to mature selfhood is motivated by the archetype of the Self.

So much for analytical psychology and the light it may contribute to human self-understanding, but wherein lies its religious significance? Where does God come into all of this? Two years before he died Jung was asked in a television interview whether he believed in God. He replied, "It's difficult to answer. I do not need to *believe*, I *know*!" In the public consternation that followed the telecast, he explained that he had made a psychological statement, not a metaphysical one. "God is an obvious psychic and non-physical fact", he said. "The *idea* of an all-powerful divine Being is present everywhere, unconsciously if not consciously, because it is an archetype".

We need to remember that an archetype is not in itself an idea or a concept but a propensity. It may be a propensity to create a particular kind of idea, concept, image or motif. The archetype Jung was referring to is what he saw as the propensity to strive for unity and harmony. This is why Jung did not draw any clear distinction between the God-image and the archetype of the Self. He saw the God-image as a symbol for the wholeness that the Self is seeking. "The religious need longs for wholeness", he said, "and therefore lays hold of the images of wholeness of-fered by the unconscious, which, independently of our conscious mind, rise up from the depths of our psychic nature".

To those accustomed to and conditioned by the transcenden-tal monotheism of Western culture it may seem blasphemous to link the archetype of God with the archetype of the Self. In Eastern spirituality, however, it is no surprise at all. It was the great achievement of the Hindu Upanishads to assert that Brahman (the ultimate reality unifying the world) and Atman (the eternal self experienced within) are one and the same. It is an identification that remains alive in the mystics of all tradi-tions, and, as observed in Chapter 1, was strikingly expressed by Meister Eckhart when he affirmed that "the eye with which I see God and the eye with which God sees me is one and the same eye".

It is worth noting that in Eastern Christianity the religious process of being 'saved', or what Jung chose to call individu-ation, was referred to as deification, that is, a process in which we develop our potential to become divine. St Paul had already reflected this in his famous words, "It is no longer I who live but Christ who lives in me". Similarly, the words put into the mouth of Christ by the Fourth Gospel are open to a Jungian interpreta-tion, for in them the figure of Christ portrays the perfect way of being human—"I am in the Father and the Father in me. . . . I and the Father are One".

Of course Jung, even though reared in the home of a Swiss clergyman, was no conventional Christian. Yet he retained great respect for what the great religious traditions had provided in the past and was greatly alarmed by the spiritual vacuum he saw expanding and intensifying due to the decay of the traditional forms of religion. "Modern man does not understand how much his rationalism has put him at the mercy of his psychic 'underworld'. His moral and spiritual tradition has disintegrated and he is now paying the price". While Jung believed his analytical psychology was equally applicable to all religions, he particularly desired to leave the door open for what he saw as the central importance of the Christian message for Western humankind. But he was convinced that it needed to be seen in a new light, and he lamented the fact that church leaders took so little interest in the positive contribution analytical psychology could make. Indeed religious circles almost completely ignored Jung while he was alive.

Jung never saw himself as a theologian and of course he should not be treated as such. Feuerbach did see himself as a theologian but was not accepted as one. Schleiermacher was the only one of the three to be universally judged a theologian. Yet there is a significant religious development linking these three together. Schleiermacher led us back to the God to be encountered within. Feuerbach then demonstrated just how thoroughly human—and humanly created—that God is. But Jung has taken us back to the creative source of the God-symbol itself—the mysterious and creative human psyche.

Whereas the reputations of Schleiermacher and Feuerbach were made by books they wrote very early in their careers, Jung became widely known only after his death, and that was partly as the result of a long essay he completed in the month he died.

John Freeman, who interviewed Jung for the BBC in 1959, was so impressed by the man that he tried to persuade him to write a popular, nontechnical account of his approach to the human psyche. Jung at first declined on the grounds he was old and tired, and was not sure the venture would have any success. He was finally persuaded, but not so much by Freeman as by a message he received in a dream from his own unconscious. He spent the last year of his life putting it together, and it was published posthumously as *Man and His Symbols.*

In 1968 a Dutch Roman Catholic theologian, W. H. van de Pol, wrote, "The discovery of the part played by the unconscious in man's existence has been a positive and lasting achievement of the greatest significance. . . . Modern psychology provides a totally new understanding and judgment of the sexual, emotional, ethical and religious existence of man". He went on to add that "the implications of modern psychology have not yet reached the general public and have yet to cause a shock in the circles of conventional Christianity".

Since Jung's death his ideas have become much more widely known. Because analytical psychology was never the dogmatic system that Freud's psychoanalysis tended to become, but rather a fluid and open approach to understanding the human condition, it can be fruitfully adapted and developed. It continues to be widely used in counselling, and many people draw upon it for the nurture of their own spirituality. Above all, it has opened the door for the creation of new spiritual paths that people have found more relevant for our turbulent time than traditional modes. Whether we choose to call it the inner voice, Atman, God, or the collective unconscious, there can be little doubt that the human psyche contains mysterious depths from which have come all the symbols by which we give meaning and worth to human existence.

CHAPTER 6

Pierre Teilhard de Chardin

God Is Evolving

In progressing from Schleiermacher, to Feuerbach, to Jung, it may appear that we have been moving further and further away from the vast universe of outer space into the mysterious world of inner space hidden within ourselves. We now go in the opposite direction, exemplifying an observation made by that unusual student of religious experience, Alan Watts: "To go deeper and deeper into oneself is also to go farther and farther out into the universe". That is just what our fourth religious trailblazer found himself doing, and he put it this way: "The only universe capable of containing the human person is an irreversibly 'personalizing' universe." What he meant was that both the existence of the human species within this universe, and the indubitable fact of our ability to think and to contemplate the universe of which we are a part, tell us something of extreme importance about that universe. No understanding of the universe is even marginally adequate unless it offers a credible explanation of the human phenomenon and all that occurs in the inner world of the human psyche.

The man behind this challenging claim was Pierre Teilhard de Chardin (1881–1955), who set out to show that the inner space of the human psyche and outer space of the vast physical universe

---

This lecture was first delivered under the auspices of St Andrew's Trust for the Study of Religion and Society, Wellington, New Zealand, and published by it as Chapter 4 of *Religious Trailblazers*, 1992.

are correlative aspects of one evolving process. Growing up at a time when spiritually based religious faith and materialistically based science were in even greater conflict than today, Teilhard had a deep personal sense of this opposition. For on the one hand his commitment to the faith in which he was reared led him to enter the Jesuit Order and remain a loyal and obedient Roman Catholic to the end of his days. But he was an equally committed scientist, who could in no way reject what empirical truth revealed. Although primarily a geologist, he had considerable expertise in palaeontology, physical anthropology, and comparative zoology. His studies completely convinced him of the truth of biological evolution even though his own church was still adamantly opposed to this discovery and was in the process of excommunicating all Modernist priests. As a student, Teilhard had been influenced by the French philosopher Henri Bergson, whose book *Creative Evolution* was later placed on the Roman Catholic Index of Forbidden Books.

Teilhard spent the First World War in the trenches, serving as a stretcher-bearer in the French army. Thereafter he finished his doctorate and was appointed Professor of Geology in the Catholic Institute at Paris. His convictions about evolution soon aroused tension in the church and his Order thought it desirable to remove him from a post where he could too readily influence young minds. They sent him to China, where he spent most of the next twenty-three years. While there, he carried out original geological research and even participated in the important anthropological discovery of Peking Man. But he also had ample time for reading, including authors whose thinking was very different from his own, among them Tolstoi and Dostoevski, Koestler and Graham Greene, Toynbee and Aldous Huxley, Nietzsche, Camus and Sartre.

Much more important, during the years in China his creative mind was formulating a breathtaking vision of reality in which his two chief interests, spirituality and science, fused into one and in the process resolved his inner conflict. It was a vision so all-encompassing that its period of gestation was understandably a long one. We can get glimpses of it from his earlier writings.

In 1926 he wrote, "At times when I am quite absorbed in rocks and fossils I experience an ineffable happiness at the thought that I possess, in the form of a single, all-embracing, incorruptible and loving element, the Supreme Principle wherein everything subsists and is alive". Apparently, his mind was able to perceive in one rapidly moving drama the vast eras of geological time. Where most of us think in terms of years, Teilhard could conceive of millions of years, and the theory of biological evolution requires such an almost limitless time scale to be possible, let alone convincing. Where most of us think statically, and see mountains changeless, Teilhard was able to think dynamically, visualising the upthrust and erosion of mountain ranges, the drifting of continents, and the endless diversification of living forms.

In 1934 Teilhard wrote a short essay entitled *How I Believe*. It starts off this way:

I believe that the universe is an evolution.
I believe that evolution proceeds towards spirit.
I believe that, in man, spirit is fully realized in personhood.
I believe that the supremely personal is the universal Christ.

In this last sentence it was the religious man of faith speaking, and that affirmation may strike us today as being in strange juxtaposition with what preceded it. Of course he was not speaking of the historical figure of Jesus, but of the cosmic Christ, a symbolic term we shall encounter later. And while this reference to Christ might have brought a welcome sigh of relief from his conventional fellow Christians, they would hardly be ready for what was to follow: "If as the result of some interior revolution, I were to lose in succession my faith in Christ, my faith in a personal God, and my faith in spirit, I feel that I should continue to believe invincibly in the world. The world is the first, the last and the only thing in which I believe. It is by this faith that I live. I surrender myself to this undefined faith in a single and Infallible World, wherever it may lead me". Here the scientific man of faith was speaking.

During the later '30s Teilhard began to put his thoughts together in what was to be his magnum opus. It proceeded slowly at first, some two pages a day, but by the end of 1940 it was finished and sent to Rome. After three years of deliberation the Vatican forbade its publication. In a private audience with one of Teilhard's supporters, Pope Pius XII said, "I know Father Teilhard is a great scientist but he is not a theologian. In one of his essays he speaks of 'resolving the problem of God'. But for us there is no problem".

The Vatican's rigid decision meant that Teilhard's *The Phenomenon of Man*, containing the textual expression of his great vision, together with an extensive collection of his short religious essays, remained unpublished during his lifetime. Though greatly disheartened, Teilhard remained devoutly obedient to the wishes of his church and of his Order. He returned to France after the Second World War, and as snatches of his thinking began to spread by word of mouth became something of a celebrity. Julian Huxley was only one of the scholarly notables who had long conversations with him. But this only led his church to forbid him to address large public meetings. Despite this ban, the French government honoured him for his scientific work: he was made an Officer of the Legion of Honour and was offered a Professorship in the College de France. His church refused him permission to accept it.

So fearful were the Vatican authorities of Teilhard's views that in the famous Encyclical of 1950, *Humani Generis*, they took the opportunity to condemn his opinions without actually naming him: "Some learned people will contend that the theory of evolution applies to the origin of all things whatsoever. Accepting it without caution, they boldly give rein to pantheistic speculations which represent the whole universe as left at the mercy of a continual process of evolution. These false evolutionary notions, with their denial of all that is absolute or fixed or abiding in human experience, are eagerly welcomed by the Communists and they have paved the way for the new erroneous philosophy of existentialism".

So Teilhard's voice was not to be heard—yet. He lived his last few years in virtual exile in United States. When he died in New York on Easter Day 1955, only a handful of people attended his funeral, and no one witnessed his burial. And not until after his death did any but a few know what was in *The Phenomenon of Man*. Published in the original French in the year of his death, it appeared in English translation in 1959, and during the next few years it became the book everybody was talking about. Scientists and theologians were deeply divided in their assessment—and not so much from each other as among themselves. It was spoken of approvingly by such internationally recognised scientists as Joseph Needham, Bernard Towers and Theodosius Dobzhansky, and the highly regarded Julian Huxley wrote the Introduction. But the geneticist Peter Medawar wrote a devastating review, calling it mostly "nonsense, tricked out by a variety of tedious metaphysical conceits". Theologians, both Catholic and Protestant, were equally divided. Some praised it glowingly, while others dismissed it as one more religious oddity.

What can have been in a volume that some hailed as the book of the century and others scathingly rejected as a "bag of tricks which could deceive only the gullible"? Part of the answer is that Teilhard intended his book to be read as a scientific treatise and therefore had avoided the use of religious and theological terms. Today we find scientists like Stephen Hawking using the word 'God' quite freely in their popular presentations, but neither that word nor any specifically Christian term appears in *The Phenomenon of Man*, except in a very short Epilogue. Assessed purely as a scientific work it may well deserve the harsh criticism of Medawar, for it lacks the precision and careful use of terms that science requires. It uses words poetically rather than scientifically and coins a large number of new words that are often used with blithe abandon. Perhaps the book is best understood as a work of art, a grand story or a cosmic vision sketched on the grandest possible scale.

Teilhard repeatedly stressed that we should not speak of the cosmos as if it were a fixed thing; rather we should speak of cosmogenesis, which means 'the coming into being of the cosmos'. He insisted that the cosmos is not a thing but a process, starting from Alpha and moving steadily towards its culmination as Omega. Alpha and Omega are more than the end markers of time; of biblical origin, they are symbols of the process itself. Teilhard loved to quote the words attributed to the Cosmic Christ in the book of Revelation: "I am the Alpha and the Omega, the first and the last, the beginning and the end".

It was Teilhard's intention to describe the cosmic process, drawing upon all that we know of it through such sciences as cosmology, physics, chemistry and zoology, and thereby to show the evolution of the human species as part of a single, all-embracing totality. Above all he felt it necessary to explain the phenomenon of human consciousness and thought, something that the pure sciences had until then simply ignored and that was to be the primary focus and climax of his story.

Teilhard made a complete break with all dualistic views that divided reality into a spiritual world and a physical world, with the former called upon to explain the existence and phenomenology of the latter. In monotheistic cultures this spiritual world is centred on God as both the Creator and the Provider whose being explained everything and, being eternal, did not require explanation. This modern philosophical dualism stemmed from Descartes, who considered mind (or consciousness) to be separate from the physical world, and as we noted earlier, lay behind Hegel's opting for the primacy of mind and Feuerbach's insistence on the primacy of the physical. Teilhard set out to transcend dualism altogether and affirm the absolute unity of all reality in much the same way as Spinoza (1632–77) before him had done.

But Teilhard achieved this only by taking that duality back into the basic stuff of the universe, which for want of any better term we still refer to as energy. But on what grounds can we claim to know anything about this energy that forms the basic stuff of reality? While some agree with Teilhard's statement that "In the last analysis, somehow or other there must be a single energy operation in the world", modern physics has given us no clear insight into what it is. We can study energy in its many different forms, and we know it can change from one form to another, but the essential nature of energy still eludes us.

To explain the existence of human consciousness Teilhard made a postulation about energy that most scientists would regard as almost laughable. Energy, said Teilhard, must have an 'inside' and an 'outside'. He used the French words *'Le dedans'* and *'Le dehors'*. It is only the 'outside' that is measurable and open to investigation by the physicist; so the physicist concludes that physical matter has only an outside. So does the biologist, though for him it is becoming a little less certain. In the case of humans, however, this approach finally breaks down, for it can no longer be denied that we do have an 'inside'. Coextensive with our physical exterior we have an interior, with which we reflect, philosophise, and engage in scientific endeavour. So at least one element of the universe, the human species, offers evidence that the very stuff of the universe does have an inner aspect. Therefore, argued Teilhard, the structure of the universe exhibits a duality in its most elemental form.

Teilhard concluded that the 'inside' begins to manifest itself only after energy has organized itself into a sufficiently high level of complexity. For example, it has done this in the higher orders of living creatures that clearly manifest the phenomenon of consciousness; and in the human species, where the highest known degree of complexity exists, we also find the highest level of consciousness.

Why has energy organized itself through aeons of time into ever more complex forms? Teilhard's answer was that energy operates in both a radial direction and a tangential direction. Radial energy, which is the 'inside', is the key to evolution, to the emergence of life and to rise of consciousness, operating by the process Teilhard called 'complexification'. Teilhard's postulation of the 'inside' of energy led him to what he called the 'law of complexity-consciousness', which asserts a direct correlation between the degree of complexity and the rising level of consciousness. He made much of the principle that 'the whole is more than the sum of its parts'; from growing complexity there emerges a new entity that was not previously there: in this case, consciousness. From this law Teilhard extrapolated the conclusion that consciousness is potentially present even in the simplest forms or patterns of energy. This is why I said earlier that Teilhard had avoided the traditional dualisms, but only by taking duality back into the basic stuff of the universe. "To avoid a fundamental dualism, at once impossible and anti-scientific, and at the same time to safeguard the natural complexity of the stuff of the universe . . . we shall assume that, essentially, all energy is psychic in nature; but add that in each particular element this fundamental energy is divided into two distinct components: a *tangential energy* which links the element with all others of the same order . . . and *radial energy* which draws it towards even greater complexity".

Teilhard fully conceded that what he postulated was in conflict with the well-established Second Law of Thermodynamics. This law (also known as entropy) states that in the course of time the universe becomes more and more disordered. Teilhard argued that this Law is true only of tangential energy, which is all that the physicist can study. It is radial energy that produces complexification and brings order out of chaos. If pressed by the physicist to defend his postulated radial energy when there is no way of detecting it empirically, Teilhard was ready with his trump card: he challenged the physicists to come up with an alternative way of explaining human consciousness. Teilhard had already invented his new terms when he came across some supportive words from the eminent scientist J. B. S. Haldane: "We do not find obvious evidence of life or mind in so-called inert matter . . . but if the scientific point of view is correct, we shall ultimately find them, at least in rudimentary forms, all through the universe".

In *The Phenomenon of Man* Teilhard set out to describe, as a grand unfolding drama, the whole of cosmogenesis from Alpha to Omega. To this end he divided the story into four sections that he called: Pre-Life, Life, Thought, and Survival (by which he meant the Future). He thus sought to find a way to explain how each successive stage could come into being wholly from what had preceded it, that all the products of evolution were made possible because of what was already there. In other words, Omega was embryonically present in Alpha, just as consciousness was already potentially present in the basic stuff of the universe.

Most of the first section is taken up with his discussion of the nature of energy, but it ends with a short description of how, some thousands of millions of years ago, a fragment of matter became detached from the sun by some accident and the planet earth was born. The earth, a product of the sun's nuclear furnace, quickly crystallized into a variety of stable atoms and the further evolution of matter began. Teilhard left open the question of whether similar examples have occurred elsewhere in the universe, but since the earth is the only one we can study adequately, it is on the earth the book now concentrates. And already within the physical matter of the earth the process of complexification was clearly at work. For not only did the unstable forms of subatomic matter solidify into the more complex, stable forms of atoms, but also the atoms in turn, as any schoolchild knows, showed an amazing capacity to join into molecules made up of different kinds of atoms and thus form entirely new substances. Some molecules have become so complex—sometimes containing millions of molecules—that we refer to them as megamolecules.

The very complexity of the megamolecule is the key to the next evolutionary stage: the advent of life, the story of biogenesis. Just how did life emerge from nonlife, and what makes something alive? An entity may be said to be living if it is capable of reproducing itself. Teilhard regarded the cell as the smallest granule of life, just as the atom is the smallest granule of stable matter. Yet even the limited knowledge available to him enabled him to recognize that the virus satisfies the definition of a living entity, and that the line between nonlife and life may therefore turn out to be an arbitrary one drawn by humans. If so, the virus may be as close to that line as we can get.

Teilhard drew attention to the complexity of such living entities as the virus and the cell. Even the virus, he suggested, may well contain millions of atoms. He saw this accelerating complexity as the key to the transition from the megamolecule that we judge to be nonliving to the microorganism that we describe as alive. "In the cell", he said, "what we have is really the stuff of the universe reappearing once again with all its characteristics—only this time it reached a higher rung of complexity and thus, by the same stroke, it has advanced still further into consciousness".

"Life had no sooner started", said Teilhard, "than it swarmed". Even today we are amazed at the tremendous number of living species, both botanical and zoological. But we now know from the fossil records that those now extant represent only a minority of the almost countless number that have existed at one time or another. And we are also aware that, largely as a result of human activity, species are now becoming extinct at an alarming rate.

In his description of the multiplication of species Teilhard introduced a concept that most naturalists today reject. He termed it 'orthogenesis', and by it implied that the evolving process progressed in a straight line—that is, evolution has been following a particular direction. Teilhard argued that without orthogenesis life would simply have spread out in all directions and there would have been no ascent of the kind that has made the human condition possible. Scientific admirers of Teilhard are divided as to how rigidly he held to orthogenesis, for he fully conceded that the way life has evolved involved a great element of chance, and that its further evolution is far from certain. He noted the many dead ends that have occurred, like the long age of the dinosaurs before their virtual disappearance. He nevertheless insisted that when one looks back over the whole process from the beginning until the present, some degree of orthogenesis is clearly discernible. He offered as evidence what he called a 'cosmic drift' towards greater complexity, and an accompanying increase in the level of consciousness.

Teilhard proceeded to demonstrate this by citing the evolution of zoological species from microorganisms through megaorganisms to land animals, vertebrates, primates and finally anthropoids. He insisted that the tree of life has a trunk, that mammals form a dominant branch, that primates are the leading shoot and that anthropoids are the end bud of that shoot. What makes the primates so important in the zoological field is that they represent an advancing cerebralisation. He said that the other animals, such as horses and dogs, "became, like the insect, to some extent prisoners of the instruments of their swift-moving or predatory ways. For that is what their limbs and teeth had become. In the case of the primates, on the other hand, evolution went straight to work on the brain, neglecting everything else, which accordingly remained malleable".

This has meant that the next stage of the evolving universe advances through one particular species, *homo sapiens*. For only in the human species did thought come to birth. And of course this brings us to his third section, the one that describes a process for which Teilhard coined the term 'noogenesis'. It means the coming into being of thought, or even better, 'reflection'. "Reflection", he said, "is the power acquired by a consciousness to turn in upon itself . . . no longer merely to know but to know that one knows". Teilhard fully conceded that the other higher animals are able to think and even possess an elementary form of knowledge. 'They know' but only humans 'know that they know'. And this capacity for reflection has opened up a great chasm between humans and all other living creatures. Teilhard viewed it as a threshold of change as wide and as significant as the gulf between nonlife and life. Yet, in spite of these two successive separations, evolution has been one continuous process with no fundamental disruption and always in the same general direction towards higher levels of consciousness.

The evolution of human reflection has meant that this earth is enveloped by a new kind of sphere. For a long time in the early stages of geogenesis all that existed was the barysphere (the solid core), the hydrosphere (the oceans), and the atmosphere (the air). Then, beginning beneath the surface of the hydrosphere and later above the surface and within the atmosphere, evolved the biosphere—the planetary envelope of life. More recently has emerged the noosphere—the envelope of thought, in which we humans live and move and have our being, and without which we would not be human.

Humankind came so silently into the world that by the time we catch the first traces of their presence they were sprawling all over the world from Africa to Peking. The evolution of human culture, while lengthy when compared with the life of an individual, represents but a brief moment in the recent history of the planet. And although proceeding at a much faster rate than the previous stages of evolution, it is still accelerating. "The human being is now discovering", said Teilhard, "that *he is nothing else than evolution become conscious of itself*". These words, incidentally, first came from Julian Huxley and were eagerly adopted by Teilhard, as he said, "The consciousness of each of us is evolution looking at itself and reflecting upon itself". The human species is not at the centre of the universe in the way our medieval forebears thought in their simplicity, but the phenomenon of man is something much more wonderful—an arrow pointing the way to the final unification of the world in terms of life. But that brought Teilhard to his fourth and final section, in which he looked into the future.

"The stuff of the universe, by becoming thinking," he said, "has not yet completed its evolutionary cycle, and we are therefore moving forward to some new critical point which lies ahead". Teilhard then projected into the future the same evolutionary trends he had observed in the planetary past, namely, complexification and a higher level of consciousness. But how did he envisage a more complex entity than the human being? The next stage of evolution, he proposed, will take place not in the individual but in society, a society that will come to incorporate all individual persons in a living whole. "No evolutionary future awaits human beings", he wrote, "except in association with all other human beings".

Because of what he called 'planetization', he thought the time was now ripe for this phase to begin. When the human species first emerged, it scattered and diversified into races and cultures. It could continue to do this only while the earth was big enough for its further expansion. Now that the finite earth has been encircled by the human species and the noosphere it has generated, it will inevitably fold in upon itself to develop an ever more complex, interdependent, and ultimately unified society. We human beings will not ourselves become more highly evolved, but we shall be part of a higher entity, just as the living cells in our body constitute a much more complex living whole. Networks of interdependence, sharing of information and willing cooperation will build a global super-society. We shall become, he said, "a harmonized collectivity of consciousnesses equivalent to a sort of super-consciousness". It could well be argued that we already manifest the beginnings of this in the increased number of our international organizations, our establishment of what we call 'think-tanks', and the world-circling web of computer networks. Teilhard, who witnessed the rise of twentieth-century totalitarianism in Germany, Italy and Russia, agreed they were monstrous evils but insisted they were in fact distortions of a magnificent possibility: an harmonious cooperative society. "The great human machine is designed to work and must work," he said, "by producing a super-abundance of mind".

The super-human society will have a centre, not in the form of a dictator pressing down from above, but a spiritual centre uniting all humankind and leading us from the future. That spiritual centre Teilhard called Omega; it will be to humanity what the spirit of the hive is to a resident swarm of bees. "By its structure Omega must be a distinct Centre radiating at the core of a system of centres". Just once, at this point, the word 'God' slips in, perhaps unintentionally, in relation to Omega. The evolving process that Teilhard has been describing from its beginning to its end is the way he understands the meaning of the word 'God'. God is the evolving process. We humans are part of it. Our thinking and our planning are part of it. The way we are becoming increasingly linked in personal relationships of love, concern and mutual responsibility are all part of it. In fact, so far as this planet is concerned, maybe even within the vast universe, we humans represent the evolving manifestation of God.

What Teilhard only hinted at in *The Phenomenon of Man* he treated at great length in his many other writings. There he uses the familiar Christian terms very freely, yet extended in meaning to incorporate his vision of the evolving cosmos. He identifies Omega with the Cosmic Christ, drawing upon New Testament themes where the word 'Christ' had already become the symbolic name for the Christian community as a whole, and where Christians were said to be 'in Christ' and urged to regard themselves as the very limbs and organs of Christ. Teilhard loved to quote from Colossians, which speaks of Christ as the one in whom all things were created and in whom all things hold together, and looks to the time when all differences of class, nationality and creed will be transcended, for all will be in Christ. Teilhard even spoke of this future age of cosmogenesis as Christogenesis—the evolution of Christ. "Everything in the universe ultimately proceeds towards Christ-Omega; since the whole of cosmogenesis is ultimately through geogenesis, biogenesis, noogenesis to Christogenesis".

What are we to make of Teilhard fifty years later? Even Teilhard conceded that "many will close this book, wondering whether I have been leading them through facts, through metaphysics or through dreams". Raphael Patai, a Jewish anthropologist, observes in his *Myth and Modern Man* that "Teilhard embarks on a mythical-eschatological fantasy voyage that easily dwarfs every previous vision of the ultimate end of humanity".

Dobzhansky judged that "Teilhard aimed at no less than a total integrated system of thought which would show to modern man that he is placed on this earth not through some silly accident but that he is the vanguard of the billions of years of cosmogenesis and noogenesis. . . . Teilhard's religion was that of a great thinker who was aware that he lived in an age of science".

With the rapid advance in the scientific world many of Teilhard's specific claims and illustrations have become dated. But his general thrust remains. At first the biologists were interested in him, but more recently it has been the physicists. In their recent book *The Anthropic Cosmological Principle* John Barrow and Frank Tipler have devoted a chapter to him and are themselves proposing 'the anthropic principle', which asserts that "a life-giving factor lies at the centre of the whole machinery and design of the world".

The state of the worldwide Christian church today is not what Teilhard would have expected, for he was reared in a time when the full Christianization of the planet was expected within a generation. Nonetheless, he was fully aware that the traditional Christian beliefs and terminology, including the word 'God', were in trouble. He set out to solve those problems. His new approach to the understanding of God as the evolving process itself has now become a part of a body of modern thought known as process theology.

In these days when we have become aware of how easily the human species, and indeed planetary life as a whole, could face extinction due to a variety of factors, it is not easy to be as optimistic as Teilhard was. And even he warned that the culmination to which he looked was by no means certain. Still he ultimately took heart not from any dogmatic teaching of the church nor from the Bible, but from the evolutionary process. Because of what it has brought forth through the aeons of time, he had hope for the future and remained a person of faith. For him God and the evolutionary process were virtually one and the same. At a time like ours in planetary and cultural history, we need visionaries of the calibre of Pierre Teilhard de Chardin.

John Robinson

Honest to God

In 1963, now fifty years ago, Bishop John Robinson published *Honest to God,* a little book that sold more quickly and widely than any theological work in the history of the world—and I dare to suggest that this record may never be surpassed. Before long its publication had reached a million copies, it was available in seventeen languages, and it has just been republished in its original form. In the whole of the twentieth century no theological book was read so widely as this little volume. Why was that so?

In some respects it remains a puzzle to this day, for it was not because the book had anything strikingly fresh to say. Those of us engaged in theological teaching at the time found little that was new or different; to us it was basically a summarised rehash of the thinking of three theologians whose work many of us had been reading and absorbing for some time. In fact, it led us to joke that it had taken an illness to force John Robinson to take time off from his busy ecclesiastical schedule to catch up with his reading.

Robinson began by asking whether we have come to the end of supernaturalist theism and sketched what Paul Tillich had been writing—first in two widely read books, *The Shaking of the*

This lecture was delivered to the annual Conference of the New Zealand Sea of Faith Network at Hastings, New Zealand, in October 2013.

Foundations and *The Courage to Be*, and later in the first two volumes of his massive three-volume *Systematic Theology*. In his own search to find a satisfying way of understanding the meaning of 'God', Robinson fastened on Tillich's definition of God as 'the ground of our being'. This, Robinson argued, showed that theology is not about a particular Being called God but about the ultimate questions posed by our very existence, or being. Next, Robinson turned to the impact of Dietrich Bonhoeffer, whose letters from a Nazi prison provided a rich collection of seed thoughts that many of us were already mulling over. In particular, Robinson was fascinated by Bonhoeffer's new assessment of Jesus as 'the man for others', rather than as a divine figure. Third, but much less prominent, was the influence of Rudolf Bultmann, whose demythologising of the New Testament had become known to scholars outside of Germany only after the Second World War. To these chapters Robinson added one entitled 'The New Morality' that expressed his approval of an article on 'situation ethics' by Joseph Fletcher.

Thus Robinson was pulling together the thoughts of a number of theologians who were then at the leading edge of Christian thought. Had he transformed the originals into a simpler and more lucid statement, one could better explain the sudden and widespread interest. But *Honest to God* is not a particularly easy book for those unfamiliar with theological literature, and indeed a number of us faulted it for this very reason. We found it a bit of a hotchpotch; his more severe critics claimed it was woolly and revealed many inconsistencies. Even Robinson himself later said that if he had known it was going to be read so widely, he would have employed a style much more accessible to lay people.

So why did it become a runaway bestseller? In small part because of a set of chance events surrounding the time of its publication. Not long beforehand, Bishop Robinson had gained widespread public notoriety over his appearance in a celebrated court case where he publicly defended the publication of the unexpurgated text of *Lady Chatterley's Lover*. Thus his name was already being bandied about in the public arena, and this meant that journalists were on the alert for anything unusual. Accordingly, the public press chose to announce the arrival of Robinson's new book with these words on the billboards: "Our image of God must go".

From the very beginning the public assumed that Robinson was making a break with Christian orthodoxy on the basic issue of the reality of God. That seems clearly implied when we read on page 13 of the preface, "Whatever we may accept with the top of our minds, most of us still retain deep down the mental image of 'an old man in the sky'". If in fact we keep talking of and praying to 'Our Father in heaven', how can we avoid having such an image of God?

But Robinson was not rejecting God, as the atheist does; rather he was calling for "a restating of traditional orthodoxy in modern terms". For such a recasting, he judged that "the most fundamental categories of our theology—of God, of the super-natural and of religion itself—must go into the melting". And as we shall presently see, he was not the first to call for such a radical reconstruction. So why the stir?

What was new about this book was that it was written by a bishop. Theologians may question and explore, but bishops are expected to be the authoritative guardians of the faith. Moreover, Robinson wrote in a personal style and confessed his own difficulties with orthodox Christian doctrines. He judged them to be expressed in thought-forms and language that had long become obsolete in the world outside of the church. Correctly guessing that his book would surprise some readers, he concluded his short preface with these words: "What I have tried to say, in a tentative and exploratory way, may seem to be radical, and doubtless to many heretical. The one thing of which

I am fairly sure is that, in retrospect it will be seen to have erred in not being nearly radical enough". Those prophetic words have certainly proved to be all too true.

I conclude that it was this personal and public confession of doubt by a bishop that caused hundreds of thousands of church-goers to respond favourably. For what came across in the book was Robinson's honesty and frankness about his own theological concerns. Indeed, many must have felt relieved that no lesser person than a bishop was experiencing the same problems as they were with the traditional formulations of the Christian faith.

Thus it is not surprising that the book elicited a torrent of criticism, much more than even Robinson had expected. The Anglican journal *The Church Times* commented, "It is not every day that a bishop goes on public record as apparently denying almost every Christian doctrine of the church in which he holds office".

We in theological colleges tended to overlook the fact that what was already familiar to us was like a sudden blast of cold air to those who had no inkling of what had been going on for decades among theologians. Theology was normally published in hardbacks and in jargon so technical that laymen generally found it beyond access and understanding, but in *Honest to God*, it was put in a nutshell and published as a paperback. Some of Robinson's critics even complained that by publishing his ideas in a simple paperback, he was making available to theologically untrained minds a number of weighty religious matters that they were not yet ready to understand.

The book gave rise to widespread debate, and within six months the publisher, David Edwards of the SCM Press, had published a second book, *The Honest to God Debate*. This con-sisted of a selection of the thousand letters to Robinson, many extracts from hundreds of reviews, along with articles by such theologians as David Jenkins and John Macquarrie, and the

Oxford philosopher, Alasdair MacIntyre. The latter concluded that Robinson had become an atheist like himself and believed Robinson's desire to restate the faith in modern terms was "a desperate attempt that cannot succeed". He thought Robinson's book simply reflected the changing face of religion in the UK and concluded with the quip: "The creed of the English is that there is no God and that it is wise to pray to him from time to time".

Yes, the book did reflect the changing face of religion, and not only in the UK but in much of the Western Christian world. One reason it became such a bestseller was its perfect timing. When we look at *Honest to God* in its historical context, we can see its importance as a significant marker in an ongoing process: it was the first of several related events that characterised the decade of the 1960s. It appeared in 1963, the year of Martin Luther King's epochal "I Have a Dream" address. In 1966, the front cover of *Time* magazine drew the world's attention to the 'Death of God' theologians Thomas Altizer, William Hamilton, and Paul van Buren. That same year the Jewish 'Death of God' rabbi, Richard Rubenstein, wrote his *After Auschwitz*. Also in 1966, Joseph Fletcher published his *Situation Ethics*, a volume that caused a stir reminiscent of *Honest to God*, and that in 1968 was similarly followed by *The Situation Ethics Debate*, a volume documenting the response it generated. In New Zealand, 1966 was the year in which we had our own very public and widespread theological debate on the resurrection of Jesus, culminating in the notorious 1967 'heresy trial'.

In short, the 1960s proved to be a critical turning point for Western Christianity. As one churchman prophetically remarked, "Things will never be the same again". The long, slow decline in church attendance began a rapid acceleration; it was as if *Honest to God* had blown the roof off the church and let in the fresh air. But though some put the blame on Robinson and others like him, *Honest to God* was not so much the cause as simply another important step in a transition that had started much earlier. To view that context we must now turn to the broader picture of the changing face of religion in modern times.

We must go as far back as 1800 or, more specifically 1799, the year in which the rising theological star Friedrich Schleiermacher[1] published a book that raised a stir in Germany not unlike that caused by *Honest to God*. It was titled *On Religion: Speeches to Its Cultured Despisers.* The latter term referred to David Hume and other leading lights of the Enlightenment who were subjecting all religious claims to rigorous rational criticism and rejecting all appeals to divine revelation.

In its day Schleiermacher's book was more radical and challenging than *Honest to God*, and yet far from being condemned by critics within the church, Schleiermacher was hailed as one who helped to salvage Christianity from the attacks of its rationalistic, atheistic Enlightenment critics. He was a hospital chaplain at the time he burst into print (anonymously at first), but before long he was appointed to a Chair of Theology, first at Halle and soon after at the newly-established University of Berlin, a Chair he held until his death.

Schleiermacher was a very popular teacher and preacher who was so highly admired that when he died at the age of 66, nearly the whole of Berlin turned out to honour him at his funeral. His thinking dominated Protestant thought throughout the nineteenth century, including that of my own theological teacher, John Dickie, who spoke of him as the most creative Christian thinker since the Reformation. Not surprisingly, Schleiermacher became known as 'the father of Protestant liberalism'.

The widespread approval he enjoyed tends to obscure the radical change in religious thought that he pioneered. Indeed, he did not himself appreciate or fully understand just what he was doing, and certainly did not foresee all the results of his new method. He was much more of a revolutionary than he intended to be, and it was left to others to point out what they judged to be his faults and weaknesses. Even Dickie was somewhat critical of him, though not nearly as harsh as Karl Barth, who perhaps justifiably complained that Schleiermacher's new theological method heralded the end of Christian doctrine. But when Barth reestablished the form of traditional belief labelled neo-orthodoxy, Dickie warned us students against it, judging it to be an unfortunate step backwards in time.

Even Schleiermacher retreated somewhat from some of his more surprising earlier statements when he compiled his major work, *The Christian Faith*. Yet the English title of that book obscures Schleiermacher's intent and fresh approach, for the phrase 'the Christian Faith' gives the impression that 'faith' is an objective thing, a set of specific beliefs. And though that is how it had long been understood, it is not what Schleiermacher intended, for his German title *Glaubenslehre* does not even mention the word 'Christian' and means literally 'The Doctrine of Faith'. This title focuses not on God, not on divine revelation, and not on beliefs, but on the human experience of faith or trust.

It was in his first two books, *On Religion* and a little known work, *Christmas Eve*, that Schleiermacher, perhaps unintentionally, led theology in a new direction. Only very slowly did that new direction begin to show itself. It was not at all apparent while the momentum of church life continued as it had in the past; it was still not fully apparent even when I was a theological student in the early forties.

Together with Hegel, Schleiermacher opened the way for three seminal thinkers whose work shaped much of nineteenth-century thought: Strauss, Feuerbach and Marx. It led Marx to become a militant atheist and expound the communist ideology. It led Feuerbach to understand religion as a human phenomenon, but a most important one on which our very humanity depends.

It led Strauss to pioneer the modern way of studying the New Testament and this, in turn, led to Bultmann and then on to Robinson. Tillich became the twentieth-century equivalent to Schleiermacher in the nineteenth century, and so to Robinson.

But what if one were unaware of those seminal years of the nineteenth century? As late as the early 1940s my theological education left me unaware of much of it. And if even theological students were ignorant of such matters, then surely in the early 1960s most people in the pews knew absolutely nothing of the nineteenth century and what it had led to—at least until *Honest to God* suddenly came as a theological earthquake shaking Christianity to its very foundations. For many church people, there seemed to be only two alternatives: traditional Christianity or unbelief. Robinson appeared to be in a no-man's-land, sliding down a slippery slope that ended in atheism.

Let me now sketch three ways in which Schleiermacher triggered off the theological changes that led to the bombshell dropped by Robinson. These three features also describe the theological situation that became increasingly common after Robinson and obtains widely today.

First, Schleiermacher shifted the base on which to engage in the theological enterprise. Traditional theology started from God and the truths that God was believed to have revealed. Like Barth's neo-orthodoxy, it was theocentric. Schleiermacher's new theology started from humankind—from our experience of the divine. Thus it was anthropocentric, and reflected a shift from the study of divinely revealed truths (dogmatics) to the study of personal religious experience. The nature of religious truth was no longer objective, but subjective.

The reason why such a radical shift did not at first seem to make much difference is that Schleiermacher and his appreciative supporters were so immersed in Christian orthodoxy that it permeated their minds and thinking as well as their hearts. Yet it was already leading Schleiermacher to make statements such as the following from *On Religion*, assertions that even today may surprise many:

> The Universe is ceaselessly active and at every moment is revealing itself to us. . . .

> The usual conception of God as one single being outside of the world and behind the world is not the beginning and the end of religion. . . . The true nature of religion is neither this idea nor any other, but immediate consciousness of the Deity as He is found in ourselves and in the world.

As we have just seen, it did not take long for Feuerbach[2] to realise the consequences of what Schleiermacher had done. Having studied for a short time under Schleiermacher, he lost interest in preparing for the ministry and turned to philosophy, particularly to Hegel. But by adopting Schleiermacher's anthropocentric basis for philosophy (though apparently unaware of his debt to his first teacher) he turned Hegel upside down. Though he never says so, he had probably read Schleiermacher's first book, where he would have found this statement:

> The desire for personal immortality seems rather to show a lack of religion, since religion assumes a desire to lose oneself in the infinite, rather than to preserve one's own finite self.

In his seminal work *The Essence of Christianity*, Feuerbach took Schleiermacher's new anthropocentric base for theology to its logical conclusion. He asserted that when properly understood for what it really is, theology (the study of God) is really anthropology (the study of mankind). Theology is the study of the human condition, of our highest human values, our hopes, and our aspirations. As Feuerbach saw it, the supernatural world acclaimed by Christian orthodoxy was the projection on to a cosmic backdrop of humankind's inner world of aspirations and values.

That is why Schleiermacher, perhaps unintentionally, opened the door to the study of religion as a human phenomenon. A direct line runs from him to Rudolph Otto and his seminal book, *The Idea of the Holy*. Schleiermacher made possible the rise of such disciplines as the Psychology of Religion and the Sociology of Religion, and his insights led to Don Cupitt and the Sea of Faith network, and more recently to progressive Christianity.

Second, Schleiermacher's switch from a divine starting point to a human one took theology out of the hands of incontestable clergy and theologians and democratised it. Theology became a 'do-it-yourself' exercise in which all people could participate on the basis of their own inner experience. This is powerfully illustrated by Schleiermacher's relatively unknown *Christmas Eve*, which was summarized in Chapter 3.

This little book is a fascinating parable of what the theological scene was to become and uncannily sketches what now takes place in the post-Christian world generally and in the Sea of Faith network in particular. Today we no longer turn to theological authorities from whom we gratefully receive infallible answers to our questions about the substance and meaning of Christianity. Paul Tillich may have been the last creative Christian theologian, though a few imaginative voices like John Cobb, John Macquarrie, Don Cupitt, and especially Gordon Kaufman demand consideration. In this twenty-first century, creative academic theology of the kind done in the past has largely faded into nonexistence. Karl Barth may have been right when he declared that Schleiermacher's new theological method heralded the end of Christian doctrine.

Schleiermacher's switch from a divine to a human focus created yet a third path that led to the modern situation; it opened the way for dispensing with the word 'God' altogether. Schleiermacher himself foresaw this when he said, "Belief in God is not necessarily a part of religion; one can conceive of a religion without God, and it would be pure contemplation of the universe". But to most people then and, for a considerable time thereafter, the idea of 'God' was so axiomatic that it seemed to be indispensable. Even as late as 1980, Don Cupitt wrote in *Taking Leave of God*, "God is a myth we have to have". Yet, only four years later John Macquarrie said in his Gifford Lectures, *In Search of Deity*:

> There was a time in Western society when 'God' was an essential part of the everyday vocabulary. But in the West and among educated people throughout the world, this kind of God-talk has virtually ceased. People once knew, or thought they knew, what they meant when they spoke of God, and they spoke of him often. Now in the course of the day's business we may not mention him at all. The name of God seems to have been retired from our everyday discourse.

In 1999 Don Cupitt made a study of our everyday discourse in which he discovered that as the word 'God' has diminished in common usage, it has been replaced by the word 'life'. He found more than 150 'life idioms' in common use today, many of them quite new, such as 'Get a life!' He concluded that since theology has been democratized—thanks to Schleiermacher—it is no longer academic theologians but ordinary people, speaking out of the experience of living, who are at its leading edge. He called this *The New Religion of Life in Everyday Speech* (1999).

Summary

The theistic image of God had to go. It was too small, too human, too personal, and too objective. 'God' remains as a symbol, should we choose to use it, that both refers to all that transcends us and points to the unity of the *uni*verse we live in.

Honest to God was a significant marker in the process by which Western culture moved from its traditional Christian base to its current nontheistic and post-Christian stance. This process started with Schleiermacher, but only in the middle of the twentieth century did it result in an increasingly rapid decline of the churches. The nature of this transition is particularly visible in the progressive Christian churches and the Sea of Faith network. The Enlightenment gave us freedom to think, and today we in the West are becoming theological do-it-yourselfers.

Footnotes

1. See Chapter 3 for a fuller discussion of Schleiermacher.
2. For a fuller discussion of Feuerbach see Chapter 4.

Adjusting to
the Challenges

CHAPTER 8

How Humans
Made God

Only a century ago the assertion that humans made God is one that most in the Christian world would have judged to be meaningless or downright blasphemous. Even today many would regard it as absurd and perhaps offensive—and this despite an April 1966 edition of *Time* magazine that splashed on its cover the query, "Is God dead?" This article brought to public notice the fact that a few Jewish as well as Christian theologians were seriously discussing what soon came to be called 'The Death of God'.

It is commonly thought that the first to use that phrase was Friedrich Nietzsche, when in the late nineteenth century he included it in his famous Parable of the Madman. Actually, the first theologian to speak of the 'death of God' was the German theologian turned philosopher Friedrich Georg Hegel (1770–1831), also discussed in Chapter 4. Though one does not hear much about Hegel today, his thinking influenced nineteenth-century thought perhaps more than anyone else's. Indeed the twentieth-century theologian Paul Tillich wrote, "Hegel was the centre and turning-point of a world-historical movement which has directly or indirectly influenced our whole century". Why? Because Hegel introduced to the Western mind the notion of historical development and change, especially in the area of

The following was delivered as the Michael King Memorial Lecture at the Readers and Writers Festival, Auckland, 2013.

human understanding; and he helped to prepare the way for the rise and spread of the notion of evolution.

How did he do this? Hegel developed a philosophical system of thought that attempted to integrate all human knowledge—of mind, nature, history, science, and religion—into a unified whole. Basic to his system was what he termed *Geist*, a German word that means mind or spirit.

Prominent among his ardent disciples were three nineteenth-century men whose thinking greatly shaped history thereafter. The first was Karl Marx, who came to interpret human history as an unfolding dialectical process moving steadily toward the goal of the classless society. The second was David Strauss, who revolutionized our understanding of the New Testament by recognizing it as a blend of history and myth. The third was Ludwig Feuerbach (1804–72)[1], the first theologian to assert that we humans created God.

But before these disciples of Hegel could develop their radically new approaches, Feuerbach had to turn Hegel's system upside down—or as he put it, 'the right way up'. Hegel understood reality to be a dynamic and ever-changing process in which the physical world and all it contains emanated from mind or spirit. Of course Hegel's philosophy simply restated in different terms the biblical assertion that God (who is by nature pure spirit) made the earth and all physical matter. But the real truth, said Feuerbach, is that spirit or mind has emanated from physical matter. The human mind developed out of a physical body and brain, and 'God' is an idea in the human mind.

Feuerbach stumbled upon this insight twenty years before Darwin published his account of biological evolution, and nearly a century before the emergence of the science of psychology. His place in the ever-evolving world of human thought may be compared with that of Copernicus in cosmology and that of Darwin in biology. As Copernicus revolutionized our understanding of the universe and Darwin revolutionized our understanding of our origins, so Feuerbach revolutionized our understanding of religion by turning the world of religious thought upside down or, better yet, inside-out. He was only thirty-seven years of age when he published his epoch-defining work *The Essence of Christianity* (1841).

Nearly two hundred years later, with our current understanding of our evolutionary past, we are in a better position than Feuerbach to give an account of how humans created the idea of God. It is a long story but one that could not be told until after Hegel. Indeed, its earliest chapter still remains largely hidden from us and has to be pieced together as best as we can from scanty sources. What we can say with confidence is that the human creation of the idea of God was made possible by the evolution of human language.

Language, much more than our DNA, differentiates us humans from the other great apes. It was no less than two hundred thousand years ago when our primitive human ancestors began to emerge gradually out of their chimpanzee-like existence by their invention and use of language. At a painfully slow pace language evolved as a means of communication. At first it simply supplemented the use of gestures, but in time became infinitely superior to visual symbols—though even today we have not wholly dispensed with them.

Eventually, language became much more than a means of communication, for it enabled humans to construct what may be called a thought world, a precious gift they could pass on to generation after generation and which thereby would grow more intensive and extensive. Today we often refer to it, or least part of it, as our culture. The notion of God belongs to the human thought world, which evolved and expanded in tandem with the evolution of language. I have written more fully about this in *From the Big Bang to God,* and here sketch only the main stages.

As languages developed and diversified, so also did the thought worlds associated with them. After the earliest manifestation of

language, this process took place very slowly but later accelerated, particularly during the last fifty thousand years. Language
began with our primitive ancestors in much the same way as it
still begins with us as toddlers—by the giving of names to familiar objects. By this means we transform an unknown world into
a known world. Language enables us to take psychological possession of the world around us. We make it *our* world.

Thus, in the early stages of the evolution of language our ancient ancestors first gave names to everything they could observe
or touch. But what could not be seen but only felt, such as wind
and breath, remained more mysterious and elusive. It could not
be wholly mastered or possessed. Take for example our English
word *spirit*, a term we still find hard to define. It comes from the
Latin *spiritus*, which means breath. In many ancient languages
the same word can mean wind, breath or spirit depending on
the context, a fact that clearly shows how our notion of spirit
came to birth. Primitive human minds imagined themselves surrounded by an invisible spiritual world of which wind and breath
were tangible proofs. And it was not until the seventeenth century that we knew wind and breath, like all other gases, to be just
as physical as solids and liquids.

To the ancients it seemed self-evident that all natural events,
such as storms, spring growth and earthquakes, were caused by
decisions made by a personal will similar to their own. Hence
this invisible spiritual world was believed to be inhabited by
particular spirits, and thus the ancients unconsciously projected
their own personal experience into these supposed entities.
(Little children still do this with their toys and unexplained
phenomena). It was by our giving personal names to the more
significant spirits that the gods came into being. The earliest
records of human thought indicate that the gods were already
well established and humans felt themselves to be at their mercy.
In ancient Mesopotamia, we find Tiamat, Marduk, and Kingu.

In Greece such beings included Zeus, Apollo, and Aphrodite; in Rome were Jupiter, Venus, and Juno.

Although we have no way of knowing for certain, it is likely that they were known by their proper names before the word 'god' was invented as a generic term to refer to the class of beings to which they belonged. And in the eyes of the ancients, the gods belonged to a higher order of being than the mere humans they treated as their servants.

When we moderns encounter references to gods, we too readily leap to the conclusion that they represent the beginnings of religion. But it is quite anachronistic and hence misleading to use such modern terms as 'religion' and 'science' in discussing a cultural age in which such concepts did not exist. For since the word 'science' etymologically means 'knowledge', and the gods played the most important role in the world of primitive knowledge, the 'gods' were just as much concepts of primitive science as they were of primitive religion. The gods were created by human imagination to identify and explain natural phenomena. They played the same role in the ancient thought world as do the terms coined by scientists in today's thought world: electron, neutron, quark, and so on, none of which can be seen with the naked eye. And then as today, these conceived realities indicated forces that humans had to respect and obey in order to thrive—or even survive.

Each tribe or ethnic group had its own way of naming the gods and describing their distinctive portfolios. They eventually added to the forces of nature gods covering every aspect of human experience—fertility, birth, death, war, peace, love, and so on. The cultural age of the gods lasted for a very long time, and in the more isolated areas of world survived until modern times. We ourselves still name days of the week after them: the Teutonic Woden and Thor, the Roman Saturn, and of course the obvious Sun-day and Moon-day.

But the time came when the gods were no longer the most convincing way of explaining the world. This time is now called the Axial Period, a term coined by the philosopher Karl Jasper. He observed that in a relatively short period between 800 and 200 BCE the more advanced forms of human culture seemed to take a giant turn on their several axes. Karen Armstrong has written a clear and full description of this period in her book *The Great Transformation.*

During the Axial Period, in five or six independent cultures stretching from Greece to China, the gods came to be questioned, modified or abandoned. It was chiefly in ancient Iraq that the transition from the *many* gods to the *one* god took place. The one unified source of power that superseded the many gods came to be referred to simply as 'God'.

The transition is remarkably well documented in the Hebrew Bible (or Old Testament). Because its various books were either written or revised during and after the Axial Period, they everywhere reflect the new age of God that had been entered. Moreover, before long they came to be understood as inspired by that one God, with the result that for some two millennia the Bible has been regarded by Christians as the infallible Word of God. Only in the last two hundred years have scholars come to accept the Bible for what it really is—a collection of documents composed by human authors over a period of many centuries. When studied with the modern tools of historical and literary research they have proved themselves to be an invaluable source for understanding how the belief in One God (monotheism) evolved out of the belief in many gods (polytheism).

They further show that between these two forms of god-belief there intervened a stage now known as henotheism, which represents the belief that each ethnic group should give exclusive allegiance to its own proprietary god, while still accepting the reality of the gods worshipped by other peoples. The chief exponents of henotheism were the Israelite prophets.

From the time of King David (about 1000 BCE) to the end of his dynasty four hundred years later, the Israelite prophets fought a continual battle with the priests of the traditional gods of Canaan. They claimed that the people of Israel should give their allegiance only to the god they called Yahweh. (The personal name Yahweh, incidentally, may have originated as that of the storm-god and was certainly associated with the sky). The first of the well-known Ten Commandments enshrines a clear expression of this henotheism promoted by the prophets: "I am Yahweh, your God, who brought you out of the land of Egypt, out of the place of enslavement. You shall have no other gods but me". By proclaiming henotheism (one people, one god), the prophets were unwittingly preparing the way for the emergence of monotheism (there *is* only one god).

We could label the arrival of this event 'the birth of God'. And just as human birth is preceded by a period of wrenching pain during which many mothers once lost their lives, so the birth of God took place during a period of great cultural crisis for the Jewish people, a time when they and their tribal God Yahweh were in grave danger of permanent oblivion. This crisis occurred when the expanding Babylonian Empire swept over their Holy Land, destroyed their holy city of Jerusalem, demolished their one and only temple, and carried off to captivity in Babylon the royal family, the priests, the aristocracy and the educated elite.

This perilous time came to be known as the Babylonian Exile, and at the time was understandably lamented as a cultural catastrophe; yet it quite unexpectedly proved to be the period of greatest Jewish cultural creativity. Babylon was then one of the most culturally advanced cities in the world, the home of skilled mathematicians and astrologers, whose numbering system based on sixty we still use on our watches and for measuring angles and indicating latitudes on earth's surface. Yet the Jewish exiles had barely had time to adjust to this highly sophisticated cultural milieu when Babylon was in turn conquered by Cyrus the Great of Persia. Under his even more enlightened rule the innovative thinking of the Persian prophet Zarathustra became part of the cultural mix of Babylon. And this was the seer who has sometimes been hailed as the first monotheist, for he replaced Persian polytheism with the worship of a single highly moral god whom he called Ahura Mazda—the 'Lord of Light'.

In this cultural maelstrom the Jews needed to sort out and reinterpret their own traditions in order to ensure their ethnic survival, and they had to do it in the light of all the new knowledge they were encountering. To achieve this they put together what they call to this day the Torah, or Books of Moses, later known as the Pentateuch. These five books proved to be the beginning of Holy Scripture and became a prototype for the Christian Bible and the Qur'an.

The Torah began by asserting that everything in existence is to be traced back to the one source that it called God. Nothing could demonstrate more clearly how the Jews went into exile as henotheists and returned to their Holy Land as monotheists, for the opening chapter of Genesis says it all. Not only does it make no mention of the name of their national God Yahweh, but here the word 'God' assumed—perhaps for the first time!—the status of a proper name. And here we find the earliest expression of the notion that God is the creative source of all that exists, the ultimate explanation of everything and hence the key to the meaning of human existence.

Instead of assuming this document to be obsolete in view of modern science (as has been customary in the last hundred years), we should evaluate it in its original cultural context. When we do so, it turns out to be one of the most succinct and imaginative statements ever composed to explain 'the origin of everything'. Indeed, we should marvel at its comprehensive simplicity, for nothing in the world of that time could match it.

Let me remind you how it unfolds the creation of the most important phenomena on six successive days in a very simple fashion, and in an order of increasing complexity:

Day 1 Light
Day 2 Space (separating earth and sky)
Day 3 Dry land and vegetation of all kinds
Day 4 The heavenly bodies (sun, moon and stars)
Day 5 Birds and fish
Day 6 Animals, including humankind
Day 7 The sabbath or day of rest

All the earlier human explanations of how everything began had taken the form of a story, as does the much older account of Adam and Eve that came to be placed second. This new account of origins was formulated as a thesis, a set of assertions. In those days before the rise of empirical science a thesis did not need to be proved by supporting evidence; it simply had to make good sense in order to be convincing. This thesis was eminently convincing and remained so right up until modern times. (Traditionalists still find it convincing, for their belief in the divine inspiration of Holy Scripture renders it guaranteed by God himself).

In short, this unique description of origins was in its own time what modern scientists call a 'Theory of Everything'. And perhaps more important, this account of creation provided the clearest possible description of what was meant by the word 'God'.

This has been a brief sketch of how the idea of the gods emerged within the human thought world and how it subsequently evolved into the notion of one God to explain everything. Just as language was the most important tool that the human species ever invented, so it may be said that 'God' was perhaps the most important concept that ever arose in the evolving world of human thought. In a metaphorical sense God *did* create a world, for in the sphere of human thought this image provided a centre, a focal point, to which everything else could be related. Not surprisingly this centralizing idea served as a foundation stone for what became in their day two of the greatest civilisations—the Christian and the Islamic.

During the many centuries in which these civilisations flourished, the idea of God exerted such a powerful role that to suggest it originated within the human mind was quite unthinkable—and for some people it remains so. It is only since about 1800 that we have been slowly coming to appreciate how we see and understand our environment through the lens of the particular thought world in which we live and which our forebears created and passed on to us. All the words and ideas used in our thought world, including the name and concept of God, were invented by us humans. Further, just as since Darwin's time we have been learning that the universe and all earthly life have evolved, so the human thought world and its many components have evolved and are still evolving.

But only since Hegel and Darwin have we been able to appreciate that we live in a changing and evolving universe. We today are much more aware than our grandparents that language, ideas, knowledge and even science are always changing. In addition, we are now even better able than Feuerbach to understand how and why the human mind came to create the concept of God.

The capacity of the human mind to project itself onto something external to itself is now accepted by psychologists as a common mechanism. The strong tendency of ancient human minds to project themselves onto the external world accounts for the personal nature of the gods, and eventually of God. And this also explains why today's most fervent believers in a personal God so often claim to know what God is thinking and planning: they are unconsciously projecting onto God what they themselves inwardly think and aspire to.

Thus a close correlation exists between a person's thoughts and the way God is conceived. Feuerbach came to realise that we project onto 'God' all the values like love, justice and compassion that we hold dear. Even the Bible assures us that 'God is love'. Further, we project onto God all the abilities that we humans would like to possess: power, knowledge, ubiquity and durability become the divine attributes of omnipotence, omniscience, omnipresence and eternity. This all shows, asserted Feuerbach, that theology (the study of God) is really anthropology (the study of humankind)—or to be more specific, theology represents the study of our highest human values and of how we can make the most of our lives.

Today we can go further than Feuerbach was able to, for with the assistance of Jung's psychology of the subconscious we can throw new light on why the transition from polytheism to monotheism took place. In short, there appears to be a psychological reason why monotheism replaced polytheism. Throughout the human mind's evolution over many millennia and its recapitulation in each of us during our lifetime, it has displayed a strong tendency towards unification. The evolving rational mind comes to abhor contradictions, inconsistencies and disconnectedness. We start life as infants with our minds receiving a jumble of sense impressions, but by mid-life most of us have organized and unified them, enabling us to become more mature, integrated selves, a process that Jung termed individuation. We come to value mental and moral integrity, and we despise hypocrisy. Similarly, the ancient mind was aware of the diverse conflicting natural forces it encountered, and was motivated to find an underlying unity. Thus it was that polytheism (gods of nature) evolved—first into henotheism (ethnic gods) and thence into monotheism (one Creator God).

We too readily forget that the really important new element in monotheism was not the -*theism*, for that had long been present in polytheism and henotheism. What was strikingly new was the *mono*- and this was acknowledged from the beginning in the

Jewish Creed known as the Shema: "The LORD our God is one". It is to be further noted that wherever the spreading monotheism encountered polytheism it had little difficulty in replacing it, while the reverse procedure is rarely if ever found.

Further, it is the theism in monotheism that is now dying. The so-called 'death of God' marks the end of *theism*. As Bishop John Robinson declared in 1963, "our image of God as a personal being must go!"—Thus we are on notice that monotheism is now evolving yet further, this time into a simple *monism*. The theologian Gordon Kaufman pointed out that the concept of God, apart from the now outmoded images, has long served us as a unifying point to which we can orient everything else and so make sense of the world and of our place in it.

This is why some scientists occasionally surprise us by using the word. "God does not play at dice!", exclaimed Einstein on hearing about the strange phenomena of quantum physics. In recent years scientists have published books with such titles as *God and the New Physics* and *Unravelling the Mind of God*. Why? Because the idea of God remains a useful symbol to point to the unity of the universe, or that which holds the universe together as one.

For much the same reason I believe that several widely read contemporary authors, in vigorously rubbishing the idea of God altogether, have failed to appreciate how and why this concept evolved in the human thought world. Two such authors are Richard Dawkins, who wrote *The God Delusion*, and Christopher Hitchens, who wrote *God is not Great*. I agree with a great deal of what they say and have no hesitation in asserting that much that is still believed and practised by Jews, Christians and Muslims should today be judged superstition—by which I mean any belief or practice that has survived from the now outmoded cultural context where it was once appropriate.

To be sure, the idea that the universe was created by a personal supernatural being who continues to watch over it with justice and loving concern has now become outmoded. But for a very long time in our cultural past not only was this idea entirely appropriate, but it played a very positive role in leading us to the modern world, as I shall now set out to show.

We may compare the evolution of the human thought world with its parallel in biological evolution. For example, the bodily organ we call our appendix has now become redundant and serves no useful purpose, occasionally even endangering our life. But far back in time it did serve the purpose of helping our species to survive. Similarly, in cultural evolution the traditional idea of God long played a very important role by enabling us to unify our experience and knowledge. Often we fail to appreciate sufficiently what power can reside in ideas. Of all the ideas that have come to birth in the world of human thought, the concept of God has been the most powerful. The idea of God *is* great. It enabled people to believe they lived in a uni-verse and not in a multi-verse of conflicting forces. The idea of 'God' came to function as a symbol affirming the unity of the universe. If one lives in a universe, one can expect to find in it some constancy and integrity.

It is an indisputable fact that empirical science came to birth in the Christian West. Was this accidental or is there an essential connection between the two? The German physicist and philosopher Carl Friedrich von Weizsäcker, in his 1959 Gifford lectures on *The Relevance of Science*, pointed out that the concept of 'God' as a single divine creator had supplied the essential basis for the emergence of modern science. It was the oneness of God (the *mono* in monotheism) that provided the essential axiom and foundation for the rise of modern science.[2]

The basic axiom of all scientific inquiry is that natural phenomena operate in a rational and comprehensible way. This arose from the prior conviction that the whole world had been created by the one super-intelligence called God. How ironic that, although the first scientists were not personally inspired by God, it was the idea of God that led humans to develop the scientific method. From Roger Bacon onwards to the many clergymen who filled the ranks of the Royal Society when it was founded four hundred years later, it was their desire to understand the ways of God that motivated them to carry on their research. The idea of God thus played a very important role as the motivator for the emergence of the modern scientific world. Before the traditional idea of God began to die, as it did in the twentieth century, it bequeathed to us the priceless legacy of the whole enterprise of empirical science. In the evolving world of human thought, the idea of God has now done its work—and a great work it was.

Where does this leave us? In this new era of the 'death of God' we humans find we are on our own on a tiny planet in a cold, unfeeling universe that has no interest in us whatsoever. Equipped only with the tools of science and technology, we must now shoulder responsibilities for our future that we once expected the heavenly parent to manage for us. We now have to play the role of God in ways we have never had to do before, and it is yet to be seen whether we are up to that task.

Footnotes

1. See Chapter 4 for a fuller discussion of Feuerbach.
2. For an account of this see Chapter 9.

Science and the Judeo-Christian Tradition

Let us first set out to make perfectly clear what we mean by science. J. D. Bernal in his three-volume work on *Science in History* uses the term science in a broad sense to mean knowledge of the natural world and then proceeds to study its growth from the Stone Age onwards. Etymologically, of course, *science* means simply *knowledge*, but in the modern context it does not mean every kind of human knowledge. It does not, for example, refer to our knowledge of history or philosophy or the arts, to say nothing of knowledge of one another. In any case, the problem of what constitutes knowledge and how we arrive at it has long been discussed by philosophers under the heading of epistemology.

So while Bernal correctly explains that modern science emerged out of the ongoing tradition of knowledge about the natural world, humans had no reliable method for testing their accumulated 'knowledge' until some four to five hundred years ago. Knowledge was usually accepted on the authority of those who transmitted it—ancient authorities, scholars, clergy and biblical authors. For a long time, therefore, what passed for knowledge of the natural world was such an amalgam of beliefs,

Delivered as the Hudson Lecture to the Wellington Branch of the Royal Society in 2004, and subsequently published in *The Lloyd Geering Reader*, eds. Paul Morris and Mike Grimshaw (Victoria University Press, 2007).

opinions and superstitions that it was difficult to separate the true from the false.

Today the word 'science' usually indicates a particular body of knowledge that has been accumulated and confirmed by the empirical method, and is more correctly referred to as 'empirical science', by which we mean knowledge of the natural world that has been tested by empirical methods. It is an enterprise that involves, not only careful observation and measurement, but also the postulation of theories to explain events, processes and observable phenomena in the physical world, followed by experiments that test the validity of the theories. Hereafter I shall use the word 'science' in this sense.

This enterprise of modern science emerged out of a Western civilisation that had long been shaped by the Judeo-Christian tradition. Those two basic elements are hardly open to dispute. But did the rise of science occur by chance, or can we discover its specific roots in the Christian civilisation of the West rather than, say, in the culture of China or India? Was there something in Christian civilisation that provided a favourable environment, as well as the necessary stimulus, for the burgeoning of the scientific enterprise? That is the question that I wish to explore here, an investigation prompted by the German physicist and philosopher Carl Friedrich von Weizsäcker who, in his Gifford lectures, contended that 'modern science would not perhaps have been possible without Christianity'.

To be sure, Christian culture is widely perceived as antithetical to the rise of science—a view that stems in part from the church's hostile treatment of Galileo, sometimes called the first modern scientist. But the belief that religion and science are at war with one another began to surface only in the latter half of the nineteenth century.

Before that time, as we shall presently see, the church often championed what was believed to be science's welcome confirmation of the truth of Christianity. The church's rejection of Copernicus and Galileo was hardly at the root of the supposed conflict between religion and science, for that misperception flourished chiefly from about 1850–1950. It owed a great deal to the furore that followed the publication of Darwin's *Origin of Species*, and found popular expression in two books: *History of the Conflict between Religion and Science* by John William Draper in 1874, and Andrew Dickson White's two volumes on *History of the Warfare of Science with Theology in Christendom* in 1896.

The context in which these books were written was very different from that which obtains today. Science was then fighting to establish a place for itself within the universities and later in the schools because both European and American educational institutions were subject to the authority of the churches. White's book would have been more correctly entitled, 'How the enterprise of modern science has had to win emancipation from ecclesiastical control'. White, himself a churchman, had no intention of disputing the truth of Christianity; what he set out to do was to separate the scientific and religious establishments, believing each had its own legitimate role to play. Yet the very titles of these widely read books served only to perpetuate the image of conflict, and unfortunately that perception remains widespread in the popular consciousness.

What was happening during the late nineteenth century was the increasing specialisation of academic pursuits as a result of the modern knowledge explosion, for only then were the sciences separated from the arts and given their own university faculty. In fact, the roots of the academic study of science are to be found in the discipline of philosophy. Even at the beginning of the twentieth century physics was still referred to as Natural Philosophy. When I was a student in the '30s, psychology was still being studied within the department of philosophy, having previously been known as Mental Philosophy.

As the sciences gradually became differentiated from the arts, and particularly from the study of religion, they were seen at first as 'the poor relations'. We need to remember that since the foundation of the European universities in the twelfth century, theology had long held pride of place as 'The Queen of the Sciences', and the word 'science' still had its original meaning.

Today we live in a very different intellectual climate. Science and religion are two different enterprises, the former dealing with questions of the makeup and operation of the universe, and the latter with the existential questions of ultimate meaning and moral value. This is why Stephen Jay Gould said, "I do not see how science and religion could be unified or even synthesized, under any common scheme or analysis; but I also do not understand why the two enterprises should experience any conflict".

We can now say that it is the function of science to help us understand the nature of the universe, including all life on this planet and ourselves as a particular species. As a continuing and open-ended enterprise on which modern humans depend for their understanding of the natural world, science provides the modality of our world-view.

Within this framework, it is the function of religion to help us answer questions of meaning and purpose as they apply to human existence. Does human existence have any meaning, and if so, what is it? Can we assign to human life any essential or worthwhile goals whose even partial achievement offers some degree of fulfilment of our human potential? The answers we give to such questions constitute the substance of religion. Religion cannot answer the questions of how the world works; and science must remain neutral on the question of values, purpose and meaning. This leads us back to our earlier question: What was there in the Christian culture of the West that led to the modern secular world in general and in particular to the emergence of the enterprise of science?

Human culture does not evolve according to any predetermined plan but rather as a result of a series of unconnected accidents. So, in searching for any relationship between science and the cultural context in which it arose, all we can hope to find is a number of hints and clues as to what made the Christian West a favourable environment for those accidents that eventually led to modern science.

The fact that science did not advance by any clear and direct route is nowhere more clearly demonstrated than in Bill Bryson's current bestseller, *A Short History of Nearly Everything*. Modern science surfaced in Western Christendom in a series of sudden advances and a few dead ends initiated by creative people, many of whom lived on the cultural margins and were regarded as somewhat odd.

This latter fact, strangely enough, is rather typical of much in the Judeo-Christian tradition from the beginning. Moses eventually led the Israelites out of slavery in Egypt, but only after he had fled into the desert to escape the consequences of having murdered an Egyptian. As a reformer and a despised Galilean, Jesus hardly represented orthodox Jewry. Nor was Paul a typical Jew, but a Hellenist steeped in the Stoicism of his native Tarsus. Thus Christianity itself originated on the margins of Judaism, and not surprisingly it soon broke out of the restrictions of its matrix.

Now within the cultural tradition that Judaism bequeathed to both Christianity and Islam, there existed an ancient stream of thought that remained largely marginalized. Known today as the wisdom stream, it reflects the wise men who were responsible for such biblical books as Proverbs, Job, Ecclesiastes and the Wisdom of Solomon. These sages were quite different from the prophets, priests and Davidic royalists we find in the rest of the Hebrew Bible; in fact, they were critical of much in Jewish orthodoxy. What they stood in awe of was the natural world;

they encouraged people to observe the way nature worked and to accommodate their lifestyle to it. But as the Hebrew language had no word for nature, they quite predictably used the word God instead. One of their favourite sayings is best translated as, 'Reverence for nature is the beginning of wisdom'. Today these sages are commonly referred to as the 'Hebrew humanists'.

Only recently a group of New Testament scholars, in searching for the original human figure who soon became hidden behind the Christ mantle that early Christianity placed upon him, have found that Jesus of Nazareth was primarily a sage. Like the sages before him he set much of his teaching in the context of what he observed about natural phenomena. These original features of Jesus, however, soon became lost to view as the rapidly expanding and developing Christian movement fastened their attention on his person rather than on his teaching.

Not only that, but Jesus' attention to and concern with the natural world was soon to be replaced by a wisdom stream from another culture. It has been too little appreciated that what became classical Christianity resulted from the synthesis of two cultural streams—the Jewish culture that gave birth to the Jesus movement and the Greco-Roman culture whose concepts and cultural forms Christians borrowed to express their rapidly evolving faith.

Nowhere is this synthesis more clearly demonstrated than in the second-century Christian writers known as the Apologists. They boldly asserted that everything that was true in Hellenistic culture was to be acknowledged as an element of Christian truth, even to the extent of considering Plato a prototypical Christian. Thus the new tradition absorbed a great deal of Greek philosophy—a word which, after all, means 'the love of wisdom'.

Perhaps the best example of this merging of traditions is John Philoponus (490–566), professor of philosophy at Alexandria, and a great exponent of Aristotle who nonetheless subjected

Aristotle to criticism in a way that foreshadowed modern science. Among other things, he maintained

- that the heavenly bodies are of the same basic stuff (earth, air, fire and water) as this world
- that they do not move in circles
- that the universe manifests change

Somewhat like Galileo, one thousand years later, he showed by experiment that Aristotle was wrong in believing that the speed of falling objects was proportional to their weight, and he therefore rejected Aristotle's theory of motion.

The synthesis of the two cultures led to a strong element of rational enquiry in the Christian tradition and a very close relationship between theology and philosophy. At the beginning of the second millennium, Pope Sylvester, a very able scholar, assigned to reason an important place alongside revelation. Indeed, philosophy became the handmaiden of theology until quite recent times, and was used both to expound and to defend the Christian view of reality. It is important for us to recall this, for as was noted earlier, the academic pursuit of science emerged out of philosophy.

And thus the discipline of philosophy that Christianity inherited from Greece seems to have been a necessary precondition for the rise of science. Unfortunately, the Greek belief in the rational basis of the natural world and the ability of human reason to discover its basic truths led to the creation of speculative systems which, though aesthetically attractive and logically consistent, sometimes had no demonstrable relationship to the phenomenal world. Indeed, the habit of rational speculation inherited from the Greeks at first actually impeded the rise of empirical science rather than stimulating it.

While some have maintained that Greek rationalism brought about the rise of science, others have insisted that it was not by itself sufficient; it needed the added stimulus of something Christianity was able to supply. Einstein hinted at this when he asserted, 'Religion without science is blind: science without religion is lame'.

What motivated the proto-scientists to ask questions about natural phenomena? Perhaps it was curiosity, or the search for knowledge, or love of the natural world, or the feeling of awe induced by the night sky. As these tentative suggestions already show, the search for an adequate answer takes us beyond the limits of the purview of science. Indeed, the motivation comes from an area of human experience that has always been difficult to define.

A. N. Whitehead described it rather well in 1925 in his Lowell lectures on *Science and the Modern World*: he referred to it simply as religion. 'Religion is the vision of something which stands beyond, behind, and within the passing flux of immediate things; something which is real, and yet waiting to be realized; something which is a remote possibility, and yet the greatest of present facts; something that gives meaning to all that passes, and yet eludes apprehension; something whose possession is the final good, and yet is beyond all reach; something which is the ultimate ideal, and the hopeless quest'.

Did science take root in the West because something in Christianity provided or prompted that vision? If so, why did it not arise more immediately? Here we should note that despite Philoponus, Aristotle's philosophy of nature was a casualty of the synthesis of Greek and Jewish traditions, and failed to leave any permanent impact on Christianity. The swift spread of Islam two centuries later eclipsed the Christian intellectual tradition of Alexandria, and in any case, many Christian thinkers of Philoponus' time probably believed Aristotle's teachings would lead to a materialistic view of the world. Until the Middle Ages, Plato's thought was the primary Greek influence on Christianity.

Plato contrasted this tangible everyday world, subject to change and decay, with the higher world of eternal ideas or forms. Christians adopted the Platonic concept of an immortal human soul that took precedence over the physical body—a concept quite foreign to the more humanistic Jewish tradition—and his influence did much to promote the dualistic world-view that became a prominent feature of medieval Christianity. The attention of Christians thus became directed to their eternal destiny in heaven rather than to the study of this fallen world, destined for destruction.

Not until after the influence of Plato began to wane, do we find the first signs of the emergence of science. In today's cultural climate it is easy to miss the revolutionary change initiated by St Francis (1181–1226), who pioneered the revival of interest in the natural world by treating not only birds and animals as his brothers and sisters but also natural phenomena and the heavenly bodies. All this is manifested in the hymn of St Francis that is still widely sung. Ever since the nature-gods had been banished into oblivion by the Israelite prophets, Judeo-Christian orthodoxy had shown little interest in the natural world. That is why the sages were marginalized. Indeed, right up into the twentieth century any tendency to venerate some aspect of nature was frowned upon as disrespectful of the divine creator.

Today Francis is honoured as the patron saint of environmentalism, but his new interest in nature might well have had little influence had it not been soon accompanied by new knowledge of the natural world brought by the Muslim scholars in Spain. In the twelfth century Christian culture greatly benefited from its contact with Islamic culture, which had reached a high level in the previous three centuries. Of particular importance for the subsequent flowering of science was the Arabic numbering system that originated in India but was perfected and spread by Muslims.

Of special interest for our topic was the way Muslims reintroduced Aristotle's philosophy of the natural world to Christianity. The Christian world-view, long shaped by dependence on Plato and Augustine, was by now under serious threat, and the recovery of Aristotle's writings set the newly established universities of Europe in a turmoil of both excitement and alarm. Thereafter it was impossible for theologians to ignore the natural world.

It fell to Albertus, followed by Thomas Aquinas, to resolve the tension; this they did by synthesizing the traditional Christian doctrines with Aristotle's philosophy of the natural world. Although I have been unable to confirm it, I suspect that they were responsible for inventing the medieval Latin term *supernaturalis*. At any rate, it is clear that Aquinas distinguished between natural truth and supernatural truth. Natural truth is the truth about the natural world, arrived at by observation and reasoned speculation. Supernatural truth, on the other hand, is beyond human discovery and can be received only by divine revelation.

This division of reality into two worlds with two complementary forms of knowledge was destined to have far-reaching consequences. From then onwards all truth was thought to be found in the study of two books—the book of nature and the Bible. This two-book approach remained fundamental for both Catholic and Protestant scholars up until the end of the nineteenth century. But after the leading thinkers of the eighteenth-century Enlightenment challenged and undermined the very concept of divine revelation, the authority of the Bible began to decline. Thus by the twentieth century the scientific study of the book of nature held all but unchallenged sway.

But for now we must return to the Middle Ages. It might well have been thought that the introduction of Aristotle's philosophy of nature at that time would become the starting point for the rise of modern science. Indeed, a Muslim scholar, Muzaffar Iqbal, has recently put it this way, 'Islam mothered the birth of a vibrant science from the ninth to the twelfth centuries. In its adolescent stage it went off to Europe and was adopted by the Christian West. During the Enlightenment science matured. Now science is returning to its Islamic home as an independent adult and the Muslim mother must adapt to its child become stranger'.

Of course it was not as simple as that. To be sure, Aquinas' division of truth into natural and supernatural elements did have some advantages for the rise of science, for the Judeo-Christian tradition from the Israelite prophets onwards had denied all reality to the gods of nature who reigned in all primitive societies and continued into Greco-Roman times. This meant that Christians rejected the sacredness of any part of the natural world. Rather, following the biblical tradition, they believed that humans had been commanded to 'subdue the earth' and to have dominion over all living creatures. And the theology of Aquinas had conveniently acknowledged that humans had the rational capacity to study and unravel the secrets of nature.

However, the uncritical way in which Aquinas had baptised Aristotelianism into Christian thought no doubt slowed the advance of science. For example, Aristotle taught that the causes of natural events were discoverable by looking at the ends achieved. He explained the falling of free objects to the ground by saying that the object in question must have within it an inherent or natural tendency to try to reach the ground. He looked for what are called teleological or final causes instead of efficient causes, that is, the forces and conditions that exist prior to the natural event.

As a result, the first steps towards modern science were taken not by the followers of Aquinas, but by those in the thirteenth century who, like Philoponus before them, questioned Aristotle's philosophy. It is surely no accident that we find them in the order of friars established by St Francis. It was they who entered into a vigorous debate with the Dominican defenders of Aquinas.

One of them, Roger Bacon (1214–92), could even be re-garded as an early proponent of experimental science. He was the student of Robert Grosseteste (c. 1168–1253), the first chancellor of the University of Oxford. Grosseteste translated the Greek and Arabic treatises on Aristotle, and they had an im-mediate effect on Bacon, who entered into experimental activity with such zeal and energy that he became known everywhere as a kind of wonder worker. He developed the outlines of what later became known as the scientific method. He believed that by observing a succession of events in nature, one could propose a general law to account for those events; this proposal he called a 'universal experimental principle', which experimentation should then proceed either to verify or falsify.

Yet because Bacon was an erratic genius who could be incred-ibly naïve, by later standards his work left much to be desired. Still, it was through his writings that the term 'experimental science' became widespread in the West. He strove to create a universal wisdom embracing all the sciences and organized by theology. What is more, it was his deep Christian conviction that spurred him on. Bacon believed that a better understand-ing of the natural world would serve to confirm the truth of the Christian religion, and that became a widespread conviction among scientists until well into the nineteenth century.

An even greater Franciscan of the following century will show why the Thomistic synthesis was destined to prove unsatisfac-tory. He is William of Ockham (c. 1300–1349), a vigorous and independent thinker who was largely responsible for the spread of a new philosophy known as nominalism.

The prevailing philosophy of the day was known as realism. Drawing upon Plato, it asserted that only ideas or universal con-cepts are eternally real, and not subject to change and decay. For example, he would have maintained that the idea of tablehood existed even before the first table was constructed, and it would still exist if all tables were to be destroyed. In direct opposition to this, the nominalists contended that the only the particular things that exemplify the universals are real. The universals, they said, are simply concepts or names (*nomina*), which have been invented by the human mind after reflecting on the particular objects observed.

The great philosophical debate that was waged between realism and nominalism may strike us moderns as very abstract and academic, but in fact the opposition between these two ways of understanding the world has been of far-reaching significance. By a route rather different from that of Francis, it caused thinkers to focus their attention increasingly on physical, tangible things and those unseen forces amenable to scientific testing and confirmation.

It led Ockham to assert that humankind can have no reliable knowledge of God other than that by divine revelation. Aquinas had expounded several rational proofs of the existence of God (mostly borrowed, by the way, from the Muslim scholars) but Ockham denied that they possessed any cogency. He thus drove a wedge between philosophy and theology and destroyed the Thomistic synthesis. For him theology and philosophy were two quite separate intellectual disciplines: theology explores and expounds what has been divinely revealed and can be apprehended only by faith, while philosophy examines those aspects of reality that can be studied and understood by human reason, and confirmed by empirical means.

Although Ockham did not draw the contrasts as sharply as this brief sketch has done, many fourteenth-century thinkers began to sense that they were at a crossroads and that nominalism would lead in a quite different direction. It was already being referred to as the *via moderna* in contrast with the *via antiqua*. The teaching of Ockham was thus recognised in his own day as a serious threat to Christian orthodoxy. It is not surprising that he was excommunicated and expelled from the Franciscan Order.

In spite of Ockham's fate, nominalism began to capture the universities in the fourteenth century. Eventually it led philosophy to become a lay, rather than a clerical, pursuit, though it would be some centuries before the divorce between theology and philosophy was complete. In short, nominalism was the forerunner of the Renaissance and the Protestant Reformation, as well as the seventeenth-century empiricist philosophy of John Locke, and thus helped to lay the foundations of the modern scientific method. As Copleston, a twentieth-century Catholic historian of philosophy, has rightly said of nominalism, 'the way was being prepared for a philosophy of nature which, while not necessarily anti-Christian, emphasised nature as an intelligible totality governed by its own immanent laws'. The leading figures of the Renaissance are known as the humanists because of their upwards revaluation of the human condition. Whereas classical Christianity since the time of Augustine had so emphasized the sinful nature of humankind as to conclude that humankind could achieve little without the grace of God, the humanists looked positively on human nature and very favourably on human ability and initiative. The vertical orientation to heaven above, which characterized the Middle Ages and was symbolized in the great Gothic spires, came to be replaced by a horizontal outlook that acknowledged the beauty of the earth and the worth of human endeavour.

The humanists began to take a keen interest in the physical world. Nicholas of Cusa (c. 1400–1464), though a cardinal, was also a mathematician, diagnostic physician, experimental scientist, theologian and philosopher; he has been described as a model of 'Renaissance Man'. He became convinced of the unity of all reality. He affirmed that all things are in God and God is in all, a theology now known as panentheism. And since this indicates that one must study nature to know more about God, he urged the increase of knowledge through empirical enquiry. His study of plant growth, for example, showed that plants absorb nourishment from the air. Incidentally, he abhorred religious wars and believed that people of different religions should live in mutual tolerance. In his book *On the Peace of Faith* he expressed the hope of seeing a universal religion emerge. He even caught a vision of a world organisation not unlike the present United Nations.

The Renaissance led directly to the Protestant Reformation, although the resulting bitter conflict between Protestants and Catholics temporarily diverted attention from the new humanist ethos; but it resurfaced in the latter part of the Elizabethan period to become the dominant theme in Shakespeare. It was in the seventeenth-century Enlightenment, however, that the full impact of humanism soon manifested itself with its challenge to divine revelation, the spread of free thought, the assertion of human rights, the rejection of absolute monarchy, the growth of democracy, and the ensuing succession of emancipations—slaves, women, coloured races and (most recently) homosexuals. These radical changes marked an era during which both society and science were free to develop and flourish.

Though he was not a scientist but a philosopher, Francis Bacon (1561–1626) is often hailed as the founding father of science in Britain. He was highly critical of the metaphysical philosophers, likening them to spiders who spun out of their own bodies wonderfully complex webs that had no relation to reality. He was equally critical of the alchemists, the pseudo-scientists of the Middle Ages, whom he likened to ants who collected obscure esoteric knowledge at random but did not know how to use it. The true scientist, he said, should be like the bee, working harmoniously along with others to amass data, conduct experiments and learn the secrets of nature. Bacon was the first to expound the enterprise of science as a systematic study.

In London in 1660 a body of men inspired by Baconian principles formed 'The Royal Society of London for the Promotion of Natural Knowledge'. Largely composed of Puritan sympathizers and with Bishop John Wilkins as its first secretary, the Royal Society serves to illustrate the still close relationship that existed between science and the Christian tradition. The architect Christopher Wren wrote the preamble to its charter, and Isaac Newton, an early president, wrote more books on religion than he did on science. Robert Boyle, the father of modern chemistry, left a legacy to provide annual lectures 'proving the Christian religion against notorious Infidels, to wit, Atheists, Theists, Pagans, Jews, and Mohametans'.

Many clergymen belonged to the Royal Society in its first century or two, since the leisurely life of a country parson provided an ideal opportunity for a scholarly person to pursue scientific research. The Earl of Bridgewater (1756–1829) bequeathed a large sum to the Royal Society for the publishing of scientific treatises that showed how the 'power, wisdom and goodness of God' was manifested in the created world. Clearly, the Christian vision was supplying the motivation for the scientific enterprise. Many books, such as *Insect-Theology* and *Water-Theology*, were published to show how the new scientific findings revealed the foresight and divine plan of the Creator.

Those who laid the foundations of modern science were all either theists or deists, a noteworthy reminder of monotheism's foundational role in the emergence of science. Because God was conceived as one invisible mind (of infinite proportions relative to the human mind), it was assumed that there was an underlying and rational unity to the whole of nature. The Christian teaching that mankind was made in the image of God further indicated that it should be possible for humans to discover within nature the creative mind of God.

Christians, of course, were not the only monotheists. So also were Jews and Muslims. Other great cultures, such as those of India and China, might include intimations of a transcendent unity, but these remained indefinite, like the vague term 'heaven' used by Confucius. The promotion of science appears to have needed the vibrant form of monotheism of the triple-stranded tradition we know as Judaism, Christianity and Islam. The Jewish philosopher Spinoza was the first to speak of God and Nature as interchangeable terms, but I doubt that he recognized how close he was to the attitude of the ancient Israelite sages. And of course, we have already noted the contribution of Islam to the West.

The presumed rationality of nature promoted by monotheism led Ockham to his famous principle, Ockham's Razor, which proposed that the laws of nature would prove to be simple and few. Its natural corollary was that in postulating theories to be explored, one should always prefer the simpler to the more complex. This also stemmed from the assertion of monotheism, since the Judeo-Christian tradition began by replacing the complex multiplicity of polytheism with the much simpler, unitary monotheism. Thus the vision of a divine power who created the world according to his own purposeful and rational plan underpinned the scientific enterprise from its earliest appearance down to recent times. This led Weizsäcker to say, "The concept of strict and generally valid laws of nature could hardly have arisen without the Christian concept of creation. In this sense I called modern science a legacy of Christianity".

Monotheism has left its traces even in scientists who today regard themselves as atheists and agnostics and is reflected in the way they unexpectedly employ the term 'God'. Einstein stated that 'God does not play at dice', and physicist Paul Davies has entitled two of his books *God and the New Physics* and *The Mind of God*. Another image of an original first cause appears in modern scientists' search for what they call the 'Theory of Everything', a law that will unify the four basic forces they have now isolated. To be sure, Christian monotheism had long served as just such a theory, for God was appealed to as the one whose power and purpose explained everything. But since that kind of metaphysics is now obsolete, the search for 'The Theory of Everything' has become its scientific replacement.

In this sketch I have focused attention on how the rise of science is related to the Judeo-Christian tradition. But this relationship, though very important, is only one aspect of a much more extensive relationship. As I have tried to show in *Christianity without God* and, more recently, in *Is Christianity Going Anywhere?*, the modern secular world itself is intrinsically related to its Christian past. The secular world has not resulted from the rejection of Christianity, as is too commonly assumed, but represents the logical development and continuation of the Judeo-Christian tradition.

The unfortunate polarisation of religion and science, along with that of Christianity and the secular world, has resulted from what Weizsäcker called the "mutual blindness of Christianity and the modern world". So great has been the cultural change taking place with the advent of modernity that even religion's self-manifestation has been undergoing radical change. Certainly the modern secular world stands in such strong contrast to the so-called 'ages of faith' that characterized medieval times, that earlier definitions of religion and faith have proved far too narrow. My favourite definition of religion is that of Carlo della Casa, an Italian scholar: "Religion is a total mode of the interpreting and living of life". Such an understanding of religion gives us every reason to believe that people today are neither more nor less religious than those of the past.

We do well to ponder the words of Weizsäcker: "the church was blind to the true nature of modern times; the modern world was equally blind to its own nature. Both are blind to the significance of secularisation. The modern world was the result of the secularisation of Christianity".

CHAPTER 10

Idolatry in
the Church

The essence of idolatry is to worship or to treat as divine anything that is less than God. An idol is something finite that we can have mastery over because we can control, possess or at least understand it; it is a replacement for that which we find infinite or beyond our grasp. The prohibition of idolatry has long been a foundation stone of the Judeo-Christian tradition, being explicitly stated in the first two of the Ten Commandments. There it was specifically directed against the worship of graven images, but as John Robinson pointed out in *Honest to God*, the idols worshipped today are not so likely to be '*metal* images' as '*mental* images'. Thus an idol may be an idea, a concept, a dogma or an ideology to which we attribute an ultimacy or absoluteness it does not deserve.

Idols are created by the human mind, as the Protestant Reformer John Calvin declared: "The human mind is a perpetual forge for the making of idols". We create idols to provide ourselves with a sense of safety and security in a changing and uncertain world, but they turn out to be forms of self-deception that have the capacity to blind and imprison our minds. Idolatry is dangerous and destructive, for it leads to dehumanising behaviour and, in extreme cases, to mindless fanaticism.

This lecture was first delivered under the auspices of St Andrew's Trust for the Study of Religion and Society, Wellington, New Zealand, and published by it as Chapter Two of *New Idols for Old*, 1996.

Many will be surprised to hear it suggested that there is idolatry in the church. Surely the church should be the last place where one will find idols, especially since the prohibition was built into the foundation of the Judeo-Christian cultural tradition. Sadly, the Christian tradition has again and again allowed idolatry to raise its head with the result that reforming Christians have been led time and again to cleanse their tradition of this gross aberration.

But the process of recognising idols for what they are and taking action to eliminate them is not as simple as it may sound. The growth of idolatry can be so slow and subtle that idolatrous practices can long go unrecognised. And since the business of distinguishing between God and idols is much the same as that of separating genuine religion from superstition, let us start there.

Even the ancient Romans distinguished between religion and superstition; indeed we have inherited both of these terms from Latin. The basic meaning of the word *religio* can be defined as 'a conscientious concern for what really matters'. In true religion the emotions, cultural knowledge and the faculty of human reason are all in reasonable harmony. The beliefs, practices and rational reflection of a truly religious person form a cohesive whole. By contrast, the etymology of the word *superstitio* suggests something 'stands over' a person and causes a sense of dread for which no rational grounds exist. In short, superstitions are in fundamental conflict with reason. Let me now stretch that etymology a little further to define superstition as any belief or practice that no longer has any rational basis, but persists because—to parse the phrase another way—it 'stands over', or has survived from, a cultural context in which it could be deemed reasonable. Therefore, the relationship between religion and superstition may be concisely expressed thus: the superstitions of today are often the religious practices and beliefs of yesterday, just as the religious practices of today may well become the superstitions of tomorrow.

The centuries between 800 and 200 BCE have come to be known as the Axial Period because the evolution of human culture seemed to take a giant turn on its axis; that is, a radical transition occurred in which much of the religion believed and practised before that time was greatly modified or even abandoned, and was replaced by what we know today as the 'great religious traditions'. Accordingly, much of what had constituted the genuine religious forms of the pre-Axial period was judged to be superstition.

It was in the beginning of the Axial period that the Judeo-Christian prohibition of idolatry began. The idols and false gods rejected by the Israelite prophets were those that their spiritual ancestors had assumed to be the true gods. Of course it is only by looking back from this distance in time that we can now interpret in this fairly simple way what took place at the Axial Period. The elements of human culture and the events of human history are always so complex that it is nearly impossible for someone in the midst of them to see the forest for the trees. Thus the process by which idols came to be recognised was itself subject to a good deal of confusion and ambiguity at the time. This is also the reason why, throughout Christian history, any fresh attempt to draw attention to the presence of idolatry has been accompanied by controversy.

The Protestant Reformation is ample testimony to that. The Reformers regarded Catholics as idolaters and the instruments of Satan, and rejected many medieval Christian practices as dangerous superstitions. Conversely, Catholics regarded the Protestants as apostates—the enemies of God and of true religion. Much of what was said on both sides of the Catholic-Protestant rift is now open to moral and religious criticism. But the reason why the Protestant Reformation broke out at all is that radical cultural change was beginning to take root in Western Europe; the Renaissance and Reformation were simply the first signs of it. And this cultural revolution that eventually brought the modern world into being may be compared with the Axial Period that gave birth to the Judeo-Christian tradition; indeed, it is often referred to as the Second Axial Period, discussed in greater detail in Chapter 1.

This second great wave of cultural change is still at work, and is now accelerating. It is questioning, threatening and undermining the religious traditions of the first Axial period in much the same way as their founding prophets and thinkers undermined the pre-Axial cultures. And much like the first Axial period it does so by penetrating even further into the distinction between superstition and true religion, between idols and God, between pseudo-gods and the symbol of ultimate truth. Because the distinctions are not always clear, much confusion has resulted, and I can hardly hope to provide full and final answers. But I can offer one person's attempt to interpret what has been going on and to understand why certain beliefs and practices within the church are increasingly coming to be rejected as idols and superstitions.

If we remember that superstition is a belief or practice that has survived from the cultural context where it was not in conflict with reason, then it must be expected that in a fast-changing culture like ours, many elements of our cultural past can survive only as superstitions. I include within culture the particular world-view that prevails and to a considerable degree shapes our behaviour and our thinking on everyday matters. And it is clear that during the last four hundred years our world-view (that is, our mental picture of the universe) and our understanding of the human condition have both changed so fundamentally as to be irreconcilable with those held by our forebears.

In the fifteenth century it was still reasonable to believe that the earth was flat; the sailors of Christopher Columbus had valid reasons for fearing they might tumble over the edge if they journeyed too far. Today we regard members of the Flat-Earth Society as stubbornly blind cranks. Until only two hundred years ago it seemed quite reasonable to understand the heavens as the dwelling place of God, from which fitting judgement or unexpected blessings might at any time descend from the Heavenly Father, to whom all his earthly children should be rightly subservient. All of a piece with this was the common assumption that earthquakes, tornados, plagues and famines represented acts of divine punishment. Today, of course, most regard them as natural disasters. An even more fundamental change in world-view is reflected in the fact that until 150 years ago it seemed very reasonable to accept as true the biblical story that claimed the world and all its creatures originated some six thousand years ago. Today nearly everyone accepts the view of the universe opened up by modern science, a universe so vast in size, space and time that our little minds can no longer contain it in our imaginations. The long story of biological evolution is widely and increasingly accepted as the most convincing account of how we came to be here.

These are but a few simple examples of the kind of cultural changes that have taken place in the transition into modernity, changes that religion must reflect and respond to if it is to be *true* religion—that is, a manifestation of a conscientious concern for things that really matter, and not simply an outmoded collection of superstitions surviving from a culture now long obsolete.

But institutional religion, through its authoritative interpreters, has found it very difficult to respond to this cultural transition. The result is that the church, which once stood at the vanguard of cultural change as it spread through pre-Axial cultures of Europe, Western Asia, Africa and finally the Americas, now finds itself very much in the rearguard. The church has become a very conservative institution, valiantly trying to defend what it claims to be fundamental truths long after they have ceased to be rationally tenable. Let us see how some of the fundamental truths of yesterday have become the superstitions of today, and how continuing to represent them as eternal or absolute has turned them into idols.

First, let it be noted that the very word 'fundamentalist', which emerged from and first denoted a rearguard Christian action and later became extended in usage to refer to fanatical conservatives in other religions as well, clearly illustrates what I am referring to. The term derives from a series of booklets entitled 'The Fundamentals' that were published between 1909 and 1915 and distributed free of charge to every Protestant minister and Sunday School Superintendent in the English-speaking world. They came at the courtesy of two Protestant laymen of the Southern United States whose intention was to stem the tide of liberal religious thought which, in the belief of the publishers, was undermining the eternal truths on which Christianity was founded. These booklets reaffirmed the infallibility of the Bible, the deity of Christ, the Virgin Birth, miracles, the bodily resurrection of Jesus and the substitutionary view of the Atonement. In addition, they condemned the new biblical criticism and the Darwinian theory of evolution, and went on to attack Catholicism and the nineteenth-century sects of Mormonism, Jehovah's Witnesses and Christian Science.

The publication of these fundamentals led to fierce theological battles between the fundamentalists and the liberals in seminaries and churches. For example, the fundamentalists withdrew from Princeton Theological Seminary to form the conservative Westminster Seminary. The theological battle received great publicity at the time of the famous Scopes Trial of 1925, when school teacher John Scopes was tried and convicted for teaching biological evolution in a Tennessee school.

In that same year, 1925, the liberal New Testament scholar Kirsopp Lake wrote a book entitled *The Religion of Yesterday and Tomorrow* in which he made an interesting prophecy of where the debate would lead. In his view the denominational divisions of the church had already become obsolete, leaving but three substantive categories whose memberships cut right across the traditional lines:

1. **The Fundamentalists**, whom Kirsopp Lake judged to be strong in conviction but spiritually arrogant and intellectually ignorant.

2. **The Experimentalists**, whom today we would call the Radicals and among whom he counted himself. These were the people willing to shed all the inherited and supposedly unchangeable dogmas in order to be free to explore new forms or expressions of the Christian faith that were more relevant to the current cultural and intellectual climate. He judged these to hold the key to the future, but acknowledged that because they had no firm belief structure it was difficult for them to establish a viable identity.

3. **The Institutionalists**, who constituted the main body of the church. They saw themselves as liberals and were strongly critical of the fundamentalists, but they regarded the Experimentalists with dismay and opted for a middle way of affirming a watered down version of the traditional dogmas. These, thought Lake, were trying to be loyal to the old and to respond to the new; but torn by conflicting loyalties, they were often engaged in dishonest thought and double-talk.

Then Lake made this striking prophecy: "The fundamentalists will eventually triumph. They will drive the Experimentalists out of the churches and then reabsorb the Institutionalists who, under pressure, will become more orthodox. . . . The Church will shrink from left to right". That was a very remarkable prophecy in its time, for it aptly describes the current state of affairs in the mainline churches in the Western world. The Fundamentalists were a small minority in 1920 and had to fight hard to maintain their position while the Protestant churches, compared to the society around them, were much more liberal than they are today. Seventy years later it is the radicals of the mainline churches who find themselves as a small minority on the margins of church life, while the traditionalists have merged with the fundamentalists.

Why has this happened? First let us look at what gives strength to the fundamentalists. It is the conviction that they have in their possession a knowledge of absolute truth that was revealed in the ancient past and has been preserved in the Bible. The Bible is for them not the expression of fallible human thought but the very Word of God, and hence the unchangeable truth. They see themselves as the divinely ordained guardians of this truth. This conviction understandably gives them a feeling of extreme confidence and of inner power in relation to all who differ from them. They become crusaders, bent on defending and spreading the Truth as divinely revealed to them. They have a strong distrust of human reasoning and of all ideas and theories that conflict with the biblical truth, and they reject most modern biblical scholarship on the grounds that it is imposing man-made ideas and theories on the eternal Word of God.

Of course they are right to fear modern biblical scholarship, for it completely undermines their position. During the last two hundred years more intensive and critical study of the Bible has taken place than in the previous eighteen hundred. The Bible has become the most closely studied book of all time, and the result has brought home to us how completely human the book is. To understand it adequately its various sections must be set within the cultural contexts within which they were written, for every part of the Bible reflects the human culture in which it originated. The Bible may rightly be judged a great literary achievement, indeed a very noble achievement, but nevertheless a human achievement. It contains a good deal of wisdom together with a considerable admixture of much that now has little religious value, but it is still human wisdom.

It is ironic that fundamentalists find themselves in this paradoxical situation. They are strongly critical of human reason and often reject human ideas and theories of the present, but it is the ideas and beliefs of *ancient humans* they have raised to the status of absolute and divine authority. As soon as modern scholarship had shown the Bible to be a product of human origin, it had to be removed from the high pedestal on which it had come to be placed. The Bible strongly condemns idolatry and yet fundamentalists have turned the Bible into an idol. To regard it as the absolute voice of authority is in fact idolatry.

The kind of idolatry manifested by the fundamentalist Jew, Christian or Muslim clearly illustrates what is wrong with all idolatry. It becomes a form of self-imprisonment. It closes the mind and restricts the eye of the intellect to a kind of tunnel vision. It takes away one's freedom to think for oneself. It hinders mental and spiritual growth. It prevents one from becoming the mature, balanced, self-critical person each of us has the potential to become. Far from being the guardian of true religion, it is a seductive trap, for true religion, especially in its Jewish and Christian forms, originally claimed to be leading people from bondage to freedom.

Though the idolising of the Bible, sometimes called bibliolatry, is most clearly to be observed in fundamentalists or biblical literalists, it is by no means absent from the church in general, though there it often takes a more subtle form. The church has shown a great reluctance to acknowledge openly that the Bible, being of human authorship, reflects human fallibility. In view of the sort of critical appraisal found in today's cultural context, the church must acknowledge that in some matters the Bible is wrong and has become a blind guide; and this applies not only to questions of historical evidence but even more seriously to vital issues in religion and ethics.

For example, churches in Europe, America and New Zealand are currently greatly exercised over issues related to homosexuality. There is little doubt that the Bible strongly condemns homosexuality and regards it as a wicked perversion of human sexuality. Liberal Christians often try to avoid these harsh judgements by resorting to all sorts of subtle interpretations of the text to show that the Bible does not quite mean what it says. What needs to be acknowledged clearly and unambiguously is that in the light of modern knowledge of human sexuality, the Bible is morally wrong on this issue, just as it has already been shown to be historically wrong in its account of human origins and ethically wrong on the issue of slavery.

The church has been extremely slow to absorb the full implications of nineteenth-century revolution in our understanding of the Bible. This revolution led to one public furore after another in the latter half of the century as Christian scholars said such things as, "The Bible must be interpreted like any other book", or "Any true doctrine of the inspiration of the Bible must conform to all well-ascertained facts of history or of science", or "Whoever was the first dogmatist to make the terms 'the Bible' and 'the Word of God' synonymous rendered to the cause of truth and of religion an immense disservice". Yet now that these theological battles have been largely forgotten, the church all too often carries on as if no revolution had ever taken place. In both Sunday sermons and theological colleges the content of the Bible is studied and treated as if it possesses and rightfully wields some special authority over our lives and our thinking.

The Bible is a set of human writings that have been enormously influential, for as the primary extant witness to Judeo-Christian origins it is indispensable for an understanding of the Christian tradition. We rightly value the Bible, but it must be read in the light of the values we hold today and in the light of our most reliable knowledge. To expect the scriptures to provide a divine oracle pronouncing the final and infallible word on all matters religious and ethical is to make an idol of the Bible. To say "The Bible teaches . . ." as if that clinches the argument and leaves nothing more to be said, is to idolise and give unwarranted authority to the thoughts of our ancient spiritual ancestors.

Few theologians and almost no church authorities have had the courage to say what Tom Driver, theological professor in Union Seminary New York, wrote in 1981: "The terrible price Christianity has paid for the maintenance of a sacred canon [of Holy Scripture] is to have ended up with a sacred cow. . . . The Bible as sacred cow requires constant feeding, care and obeisance."

How did this cow achieve sacred status? The process was a very long and slow one. From the time the earliest sections of the Bible were composed until it was finally declared by the church to be a closed canon of Holy Scriptures, some fifteen hundred years had passed. At no point were any of the authors, nearly all of them anonymous, aware that their words would eventually be canonised as Holy Scripture.

When we seek to understand why their words were eventually given the status of the eternal Word of God, we discover another idol lying behind the idol of the Bible, one more subtle and dangerous because it is not an object but an idea: the idea of divine inspiration. In the ancient world the earliest known prophets used music and dance to work themselves up into such states of ecstasy that in a state of impaired consciousness strange words and voices came from them, and these were interpreted by onlookers as divine voices. The phenomenon was not unlike that of glossolalia, or speaking in tongues, that occurs in contemporary Pentecostalism, and that was in many ways its prototype.

From these somewhat crude and primitive origins came the notion that the Israelite prophets were as spokespersons for God; it was not their own words they uttered, but the Word of God. That is why so many of the oracles in such books as Amos and Isaiah portray God speaking in the first person. In a similar way the Qur'an, the whole of which was uttered by Muhammad over a considerable period of time, is regarded by Muslims not as the Prophet's composition, but as the pure and unadulterated pronouncements of Allah.

This belief in divine inspiration, which originally referred to the oracles of the prophets, was gradually extended to all the writings that eventually came to be regarded as sacred. The concept of divine inspiration thus came to be associated by Jew, Christian and Muslim with their respective Holy Scriptures and has remained so right down to the present, or at least until nineteenth-century Christian and Jewish scholars began to question it. And even today, any Muslim who dares to question openly the divine authority of the Qur'an is likely to find himself in the company of Salman Rushdie. Thus it happened that insights originally thought to have been divinely inspired came to be treated as divinely revealed truth and at last regarded as the eternal Word of God.

The church must surrender the belief in divine revelation, but is reluctant to do so, since that would remove the very basis on which the church has tried in the past to speak with unique and absolute authority. In today's world, however, there is no valid reason for the church to claim that it possesses an exclusive avenue to truth or a body of revealed truth to which all other claims to truth must conform. The church, including all theologians, bishops and the Pope himself, is as human and fallible as any other institutions. Not only does the church have no special knowledge of history, geology and economics, but it is also no less fallible than others on questions of religion, God and the ultimate meaning of life. For the church to claim sole guardianship of a divinely revealed body of truth is an act of idolatry; indeed, the concept of divine revelation is yet another idol that must be abandoned.

But what then becomes of all the dogmatic claims made by the church? What happens to its traditional body of teaching that supposedly goes back to Jesus and the Apostles? What of the great body of lore summarised in the creeds and expounded in great theological tomes? Does not the church know more about God than anybody else? Is not the teaching of the church the proclamation of what God has revealed to mankind? Is not this revelation uniquely to be found in Jesus Christ? What happens to all of this if the concept of divine revelation is discarded as an idol?

One cannot doubt that surrendering the appeal to divine revelation will result in sweeping changes to what is commonly called Christian teaching. Some of these changes have already begun to take place, often without people realising what is happening. Christian preaching today places far less emphasis on the supernatural, divine intervention and life beyond the grave than it once did, and far more on ethics, social justice and how to make the most of this life. But the changes are far too slow and cosmetic. If at last the idol of divine revelation were banished, then all of Christian doctrine—however reassuring, however convincing—will come to be acknowledged as essentially human teaching.

All knowledge, not only scientific but also moral and religious, remains human in origin and nature. To exalt it to some higher status is to idolise it. The value of Christian teaching must be judged not by appeal to divine revelation but to its own inherent capacity to win conviction and obedience. From now on both moral and religious teaching must stand on its own merits. Even such so-called teachings of Jesus as we find in the Sermon on the Mount must be valued not because they were spoken by Jesus Christ, but for their inherent capacity to convey to us the ring of truth. It was this compelling quality in the teaching of Jesus that first earned the attention and loyalty of his followers. Only after his death did that attention shift from the message to the messenger, with the result that the messenger became the message.

That brings us to another example of idolatry, this time with reference to the central figure of Christianity, Jesus Christ. In 1835 David Strauss published his epoch-making book, *The Life of Jesus Critically Examined*, mentioned in Chapter 4. In 1964, Bishop Stephen Neill rightly judged this book to be "a turning point in the history of the Christian faith". And ever since that book was published, it has been necessary to distinguish between what we now refer to as 'the historical Jesus' and 'the Christ of faith'.

The historical Jesus is the Jewish man of Galilee who taught, healed the sick and was crucified by the Romans. It is almost certain that there was such an historical figure, the early memories of whom formed the basis of Christian teaching. Today it is widely acknowledged by New Testament scholars that it is not possible to write a biography of Jesus, for we lack the necessary historical data. The historical person has largely eluded modern historical research, except in faintest outline, for the extant traces of him very soon became hidden behind the biblical portraits of the Christ of faith.

The Christ of faith is a divine figure whose image was conceived and developed in the collective mind of the first few generations of Christians, whose devotion and creative imagination clothed the human Jesus with divine status and described him as the divine Son of God, Saviour of the world and, eventually, the second Person of the Holy Trinity. Christians may reasonably continue to draw encouragement and inspiration from the Christ of faith, provided they acknowledge this personification to be a figure of vivid symbolic imagery. Indeed, this is the image that is so vividly dramatized by the biblical accounts (now commonly categorised as myths) of Jesus' resurrection, ascension into heaven and place of honour at the right hand of God.

As Martin Kähler made clear in his seminal book *The So-called Historical Jesus and the Historic Biblical Christ* (1896), it is not the historical Jesus who stands at the centre of the Christian tradition, but the Christ figure of the Bible, for this latter figure and the symbolic poetic imagery that goes with it constitute the spiritual motivation of the Christian tradition. The Christ of faith neither walked the dusty roads of Galilee as the historical Jesus did nor does 'he' reside in some cosmic heaven above, but rather exists as a spiritual reality in the collective imagination of the Christian community. Even St Paul conceived Christ in this way: that is why he could speak of the church as 'the body of Christ' and of Christ dwelling within the Christian.

As the theologian Gordon Kaufman has pointed out, "through most of Christian history the image of Christ was reified to the point of idolatry". The deification of Jesus by which he became the Christ-symbol can now be seen to be open to the charge of idolatry, as Jews and Muslims quite rightly pointed out long ago. Today's Progressive Christian theologians also recognise this error and call it Jesusolatry. To quote Kaufman again, "From early on Jews and Muslims realised that Christians were falling into idolatrous attitudes towards Christ and the Church, and they criticised these in the name of the One High God. But to this day Christians have seldom acknowledged this quite proper theological critique of their reified use of the central religious symbols".

The continued use of the Christ-symbol in the Christian tradition avoids the charge of idolatry only when it is acknowledged to be a symbolic image. Of course and of necessity, nearly all religious language is symbolic in one way or another, and we shall presently see this is particularly the case with the basic term 'God'. Just as it is necessary to distinguish between the historical Jesus and the Christ of faith, so it has become necessary in the modern world to distinguish between descriptive language and evaluative language. The language of scientific and historical discourse describes and deals with tangible objects, and what is asserted or described in such discourse is subject to public verification. Religious language, on the other hand, is mostly of the evaluative kind, and therefore a great deal more subjective, for it is used to express, often symbolically or poetically, what is valuable and meaningful to the speaker or to the community that shares those values.

All this may now be illustrated by turning to the concept of 'God'. All God-talk is symbolic and is expressed in evaluative language, asserting what an individual or a community believes to be of greatest value or meaning to them. The world-view in which invisible supernatural spiritual beings called gods were believed to exist received its first iconoclastic blow during the first Axial Period. The word 'God'—a term that originated as a generic reference to the class of spiritual beings with personal names—survived that radical transition, but it came to be used in a new way. The transition began with the early biblical convention of referring to 'the God of . . .'—as in 'the God of Abraham', 'the God of Moses', and so on. In other words, 'God' was employed to symbolize everything that was of ultimate importance to Abraham or Moses. In such a context 'God' was not a personal name, but a concept, a symbol.

Unfortunately, during the transition from the gods to the One God the personal traits associated with the gods were transferred to the One God, and thereafter 'God' came to be understood as a proper name. In the minds of the faithful, God was the name of an objective supernatural person—the Supreme Being. Of course, it was still strictly forbidden to portray God in visible form, though Michelangelo later did so on the ceiling of the Sistine Chapel. How he achieved that without criticism is a mystery, for already the authoritative theologian Thomas Aquinas had said, "God has no body". Only in more modern times has the symbolic nature of 'God' come to be fully recognised. Francis Bacon took a major step in this direction by pointing out in his 'Idols of the marketplace' that we fall into the error of idolatry when we use abstract terms as if they were the names of real entities and do not acknowledge them to be the human creations and fictions they are. 'God' should be understood as an abstract term, a concept, a symbol; and we become guilty of idolatry if we treat it as the personal name of some objective (albeit spiritual?) being. Even mental images and verbal descriptions of God are now subject to the charge of idolatry if they imply some objective reality.

In the twentieth century all forms of objectifying God came to be recognized as idolatry. That is why the 1960s came to be called the 'Death of God' decade. That is why the twentieth century has been marked in the Western world by widespread disbelief in the traditional understanding of God. The modern atheist who protests that no supernatural being called God actually exists is wholly justified. To affirm the existence of an objective God is to be guilty of idolatry. Those who are most convinced they actually know the mind and will of this supposed divine person open themselves to the charge that they have, however unwittingly, projected their own ideas and aspirations on to that God and then claimed divine authority for what they themselves wish to affirm and to do.

What has happened in this century is the logical conclusion of the protest against idolatry renewed four hundred years ago by Protestantism. As Driver has said, "The church has been very slow to perceive that it cannot survive the revolution in modern conscience while holding on to the notion of God as an absolute, extraneous authority, much less the Bible as the expression of that authority".

Already at the time of the Reformation Martin Luther had said, "Whatever your heart clings to and confides in, that is really your god." Paul Tillich, following and extending Luther's affirmation, refers to God as the symbol for whatever deserves to concern us in an ultimate way. Don Cupitt has said, "God is the mythical embodiment of all that one is concerned with in the spiritual life". Gordon Kaufman points out that in our language and cultural heritage the word 'God' has served us well as an ultimate point of reference, in terms of which we may understand ourselves and our world. In all these the word 'God' remains an abstract term that has meaning but no objective content. If we assign either visible or mental content to the term, content that we can no longer examine critically, we have turned God into an idol of our own making.

Kaufman has summed up the problem: "What can it mean to speak of God in a world believed to have issued from a 'big bang' fifteen billion years ago, a world in which entropy may well have the last word? . . . Most contemporary theological reflection has almost completely ignored this task, and . . . made it possible for dangerously idolatrous uses of [the concept of] 'God' to persist into modern times, uses which have helped to create the ecological crisis we face today".

The situation of Christian orthodoxy today is not unlike that faced by the ancient Israelites as Moses led them through the wilderness. Suffering hunger in the desert, fearing they would never reach the Promised Land, and longing to return to the fleshpots of Egypt, Aaron the priest (so it is said) made for them a golden calf to worship that it might bring them some reassurance to overcome their fear of the future. When Moses saw this idol he smashed it to pieces. Similarly, the Christian churches of today face an unknown future, and are strongly tempted to turn back to past tradition and raise up Christian orthodoxy and its various symbolic terms into objective idols that must be preserved and worshipped at all cost in the hope that they will bring deliverance. The time has come for the church, like Moses of old, to abandon and destroy its idols.

We should take to heart the homely advice in the Sermon on the Mount. Jesus said, "To avoid hypocrisy, you must first take the log of wood out of your own eye before you will be able to see clearly to take the speck out of your neighbour's eye". Only when the church and its theologians are prepared to acknowledge and abandon their own idols are they in a position to point out the idols in society.

Yet how is this to be done? To denounce the idols of their day the Israelite prophets were prompted by a voice they identified as God's. To what criteria can we appeal for the condemnation of idolatry, if God is no more than a symbol? Neither divine revelation nor some high moral ground of special privilege will do. Rather, the strongest appeal comes from what is now popularly referred to as a level playing field—that is, on the basis of our common humanity. It will still be the experience of some kind of voice, but an inner voice rather than a supernatural one. Some still refer to that voice as God's; others may prefer to call it conscience, human reason or common sense. Perhaps none of these terms will prove universally acceptable, but that is what we should expect when we are all part of a changing process in which culture, religion, language and thought are themselves undergoing rapid change.

What we can do is to draw from whatever cultural heritage has shaped us the honesty and courage to acknowledge our common humanity. Then we can join together in mutually respectful dialogue and acknowledge the fallibility common to us all. Further, using what rational capacities with which we have been endowed, we can critically examine the things and ideas we value most highly to discover where we may be in danger of worshipping idols of our own making.

Ethics
without God

How do we distinguish between right and wrong behaviour, choose the better path of action and avoid the worse?
We first learn these distinctions from our parents and teachers,
who pass on to us their own values along with their criteria for
making these judgments. Even before we are old enough to
develop any critical thinking of an ethical nature, then, we have
already been ethically shaped by those who have in turn been
shaped by *their* parents and by the culture in which they were
brought up. We are all products of the culture into which we
born. And even though today's multicultural world may allow
us to transcend the *particular* culture into which we were born,
we can never extricate ourselves from human culture in general.
We live in it as fish live in the sea.

As we pass through adolescence we begin to question what
we are told, and either accept or modify the values and criteria
handed on to us. That is a natural part of the process of 'coming
of age' and assuming a responsible place in society. In the process
of evolving every human culture develops the customs, principles and moral rules deemed necessary for the harmony and
well-being of the group. Our words 'morality' and 'ethics' come
from the Latin *mores* and the Greek *ethos*, words that referred to

---

Lecture delivered to the Australian Sea of Faith Conference, Queensland,
September, 2010.

the established cultural customs of Rome and Greece, and thus reflect the ongoing evolution of all cultural norms.

Now let us project this coming-of-age process onto an historical time scale. Just as individuals undergo a maturing process, so in the last three centuries a similar mutation has been occurring in human culture as a whole. Indeed, Dietrich Bonhoeffer perceptively referred to recent history as the time of 'mankind's coming of age'. How did it come to be so?

The eighteenth-century period known as the Enlightenment is widely recognized as a watershed of cultural change that presently affects all cultures of the world, though obviously in varying degrees. Unfortunately, the full significance of the Enlightenment has yet to be widely understood and appreciated, for at the popular level many still live under pre-Enlightenment conditions. This is particularly the case in those traditional Christian, Jewish and Muslim circles where moral laws inherited from the past are still regarded as eternal and unchangeable, and hence not to be questioned.

Let me briefly explain. In pre-Enlightenment monotheistic cultures it was taught by religious authorities and accepted without question that all standards of right and wrong originated with God, who ordained them and revealed them to humans. For the Jew these were set out in the Torah, for the Christian in the Bible, and for the Muslim in the Qur'an. Although some specific laws were to be found in such statements as the Ten Commandments and the Sermon on the Mount, each tradition over time drew up ethical codes of behaviour that carried the stamp of divine authority. The Jews, for example, found 613 specific commandments in their Bible, the Muslims assembled the Shari'ah, and the Christian theologians expounded an often quite complex Christian Ethic on the basis of what they found in the Bible. All of these ethical codes were considered immutable and not open to debate. It was sufficient for the church to declare, 'The Bible teaches . . .' and that was the end of the matter.

Nietzsche, that intriguing prophet of the New Age, called this approach to right behaviour 'slave morality'. To understand that charge we need only recall how we used to learn both morality and the Christian truths by memorising the catechism. Like a ventriloquist's dummy we simply repeated what others put into our mouths! Indeed, only in my childhood days was the use of the catechism as a means of instruction in religion and morals at last beginning to disappear.

The change had begun during the Enlightenment. Starting in the Christian West and slowly spreading round the globe, the human race began to move out of its childhood phase and enter that of mature adulthood. Just as political power was undergoing a transition from absolute monarchy to democracy, so the seat of religious and moral authority was shifting from a point external to us to a point within us. In religion we increasingly speak of the voice of God within us, and less and less of the God up there.

The philosopher Immanuel Kant (1724–1804) put it this way: "The Enlightenment is man's exodus from indoctrination. Indoctrination prevents one from using his own understanding. . . . 'Dare to be wise' *(sapere aude)*. Have the courage to think for yourself; this is the motto of the Enlightenment".

During the 250 years on this side of the Enlightenment the new freedom to think critically not only advanced the enterprise of modern empirical science, but also made discoveries that undermined what had long been assumed to be the firm foundations of the Christian tradition.

First came the discovery that Christian doctrine, long taken to be the deposit of divine revelation, was after all quite *human in origin*. Its construction was entirely the work of humans, having begun largely with Paul and continued through such thinkers as Augustine, Aquinas, and the Protestant reformers. Those people sincerely believed, of course, that they were simply expounding the eternal truths that were contained in the Bible.

Attention then turned to the critical examination of the Bible itself. More and more did it become clear that the Bible also is a set of *human* documents that could no longer be regarded as a collection of timeless truths that originated with God; rather they were humanly composed writings that reflected the historical and cultural context in which they were written—as well as the ignorance and the prejudices of their authors.

The next discovery concerned the *nature of the God* who had supposedly revealed his word in the Bible. Kant conceded that the reality of God could not be confirmed by any rational process, but to do justice to human experience he found it necessary to postulate both the reality of God and the immortality of the human soul. He said, "Two things fill the mind with ever new and increasing admiration and awe, the oftener and the more steadily we reflect on them: *the starry heavens above and the moral law within*".

What impressed Kant most was the universal human experience of acknowledging moral duty; he called it the 'the moral imperative'. Notice that he was now using the reality of ethics to support the reality of God, and not the other way round as had been done previously. It fell to Nietzsche to announce the demise of God. This he did most tellingly in his now famous parable of the madman. What Nietzsche had rightly discerned going on within Christendom was that the idea of God as an all-encompassing supernatural being was losing its power to convince. But what Nietzsche also realised, and sought to draw everybody's attention to, was the fact that the loss of such a God had more far-reaching consequences than at first seemed to be the case.

For not only would the whole system of Christian doctrine come tumbling down, but the long accepted foundation of all morality would also disappear. At this point it is instructive to go back to one of Kant's young disciples who has largely been lost to sight. Johann Fichte (1762–1814) was influenced by both Spinoza and Kant, but unlike Kant he found no need to postulate the existence of a divine entity (God) on the basis of the moral imperative. For him the moral order and God were virtually one and the same. "We do not and cannot grasp any other God", he said. As Fichte saw it, the moral imperative we experience within us is itself the voice of God, and when we obey it the Divine becomes alive and real in us. Thus for Fichte, the moral imperative was not only paramount, as it was for Kant, but was in fact the experience of God.

What was happening at the time of Kant and Fichte was this: While the demise of the theistic God destroyed the basis of the traditional morality, it allowed ethics to come out from under the shadow of theology where it had long languished. Ethics, the pursuit of the Good and the study of right behaviour, now stands on its own feet and has largely replaced the traditional role of theology. This transition has even given rise to such quasi-religious organisations as the International Humanists and the Ethical Union. Still more important, ethical sensitivity among responsible people, far from disappearing, has become more lively and refined as a result of the 'death of God', as I shall later exemplify.

But how did these moral values come to be the attributes of God in the first place? How did the human moral imperative come to be regarded as 'the divine imperative', to use the Swiss theologian Emil Brunner's term?

That is a long and complex story that we are only now beginning to unravel for the first time. For at least two millennia it was unthinkable even to question the reality of God. Now we are able to write a 'History of God', as Karen Armstrong has recently and expertly done.

To do this we may usefully divide the long cultural history of humankind into three successive phases. They may be conveniently labelled: the polytheistic, the monotheistic, and the humanistic. In each of these phases humans understood their moral duties quite differently because of the quite different ways in which they understood themselves and their relationship to the environment in which they lived. I shall now sketch these phases, for they help us to understand our current moral situation.

The Polytheistic Phase

As the ancients tried to understand the forces they encountered in the natural world, they invented personal names for them, much as weather forecasters still do with hurricanes. Further, they unconsciously projected their own consciousness into these storms and other natural phenomena. This is how the human mind first came to create the idea of personal spirits and gods; they were a class of unseen beings that were thought to be responsible for everything that happened in the natural world. We can easily understand how and why the ancients arrived at their polytheistic world-view, because even today we might find a two-year-old who hits his head on the table corner turning round to address the offending object by saying, 'You naughty table!'

It seems probable that the unseen spiritual beings imagined by the ancients were at first simply *identified* with the moving phenomena of nature or perhaps thought to inhabit them. Later, however, the gods were conceived as independent beings who exerted *external control* over natural forces and processes. On reaching that stage the gods possessed what philosophers call *aseity*, a word that means they now possessed an existence of their own. From our viewpoint we can say that the gods had at last become independent *beings*, but in the thought world of early humankind they had always been so.

Each of the numerous primitive cultures developed its own version of this polytheistic interpretation of nature. In most there was a Sky Father and an Earth Mother, often regarded as the progenitors of all the other gods, each of whom had his or her own portfolio or special area of operation. In ancient Greece the name of the Earth Mother was Gaia. The word is etymologically related to *ge*, the Greek word for earth, now preserved in our word 'ge-ology', the study of the earth. Gaia's male consort was Zeus, the chief of the gods.

Thus, in order to explain what we call natural phenomena, the ancients did not ask, '*How* did this event happen?' but '*Who* caused it and *why*?' This kind of reasoning occurs even to this day. We need only observe how quickly the Anglican Bishop of Sydney jumped to the conclusion that the 2004 Indian Ocean Tsunami had been willed by God to express moral displeasure!

The First Axial Period

In the first millennium before the Christian era a radical cultural transition began to take place in Europe and Asia, though not until much later did this reach the remote tribal areas of Africa, the Americas and Australasia. Karl Jaspers labelled this period of transition the Axial Period and saw it extending from about 800 to 200 BCE. Karen Armstrong has entitled her book on this watershed era *The Great Transformation*, because it ushered in a new cultural age which, in our part of the world, we know as the monotheistic period.

For the purposes of our present concern with ethics the most important aspect of the transition from polytheism to monotheism is that the God who replaced the gods became the depository of the highest human values. These were referred to as the attributes of God in a way that had never been the case with the gods of nature, for as ancient mythology clearly illustrates, their morals left much to be desired, mirroring as they did both the strengths and weaknesses of humankind. It was only from the Axial period onward that God became increasingly identified with love, compassion, goodness, truth and justice.

The transition from polytheism to monotheism took place in the period when the Persian influence of Zoroastrianism was moving westward into ancient Iraq. The Persian prophet Zoroaster not only proclaimed the oneness of the god Ahura

Mazda, but he declared him to be wholly wise, benevolent and good; the guardian of justice and the friend of the just person. Zoroaster was the first to describe the being of God primarily in terms of the highest values. The Jewish Exiles in Babylon began to follow suit, since they identified their national deity Yahweh with the one and only God. Perhaps Persian influence is to be seen in these words from the Exilic section of the book of Isaiah:

> Arise, shine for your light has come,
> and the glory of Yahweh has risen upon you.
> For behold, darkness shall cover the earth,
> and thick darkness the peoples;
> but Yahweh will rise upon you,
> and his glory will be seen upon you.
> And nations shall come to your light,
> and kings to the brightness of your rising. (Isaiah 60:1–3)

But it very soon became clear that if there is only one God, then he must be ultimately responsible for everything including evil. This was acknowledged by the Exilic prophet referred to by scholars as Deutero-Isaiah[1], the first truly monotheistic voice in the Bible, when he put the following words into the mouth of God:

> I form light and I create darkness.
> I bring health and I create disease.
> I, Yahweh, do all these things. (Isaiah 45:7)

But if the one God is also wholly good, how can this God also be responsible for evil? The protest that almost immediately began among the Jewish people gave rise to the book of Job and later to Ecclesiastes. The problem persisted as an irritant within monotheism for two thousand years, and was finally labelled 'theodicy' by the philosopher Gottfried Wilhelm Leibniz (1646–1716). In short, the affirmation that God is both omnipotent and wholly good proved to be the Achilles heel of monotheism and a moral dilemma at the heart of Christian theology.

The problem was dealt with, first in Zoroastrianism and later in Christianity and Islam, by turning pure monotheism into a form of dualism by introducing an evil force opposed to God: Ahriman (Zoroastrian), Satan (Christian) or Iblis (Islamic). The universe was conceived to be a battleground on which God and Satan (or the Devil) were engaged in a cosmic struggle for power over humans. Throughout the Middle Ages Christian imagination saw this world in which we live sandwiched between Heaven above, where God dwelt with his angels and church triumphant, and the burning Hell below, where Satan and his fiends tormented the damned.

It was this image of the three-story universe created by Christian imagination that the Enlightenment finally reduced to rubble. At the Reformation Protestants had already eliminated Purgatory, a place for moral cleansing prior to entry into heaven; by the late nineteenth century many were questioning Hell; and during the twentieth century heaven lost its significance. We now find ourselves living in one vast physical universe, a space-time continuum. Mankind is entering the secular age.

Lacking an eternal dwelling-place for God, traditional monotheism began to collapse, for God lost his aseity, just as the gods had done more than two millennia before. This revealed that God had been only a humanly created idea, even if an extremely important one. What remained of God as a kind of legacy consisted chiefly of his attributes—the supreme moral and spiritual values that were attributed to him during and after the First Axial Period.

The reason that I have sketched this history is to show that even before Nietzsche, Fichte was moving in the right direction. Here on earth we humans are on our own as we attempt to deal with the problems of human existence. Does this mean that we are free to do as we like? Not for a minute! We remain subject to a moral imperative, but it is one that arises within us as we learn—to our own ultimate benefit, rather than to please an unseen benefactor—how to relate to one another and to the world at large. The moral situation in which we find ourselves is not less demanding, but more so; for we not only have to *do* what is right but we first have to *determine* what *is* right. We have to enunciate the ethical demands that for so long we assumed to be the prerogative of God.

It was with this realization that Nietzsche not only proclaimed the death of God but also set out to define the new ethic. Recalling that Zoroaster (the Latin form of Zarathustra) seems to have been the first to describe God in terms of moral values, it is interesting to find that Nietzsche chose the name Zarathustra for the prophet who would pioneer the form of the new ethical challenges. Nietzsche was more of a sage than a philosopher. Just as such ancient sages as Ecclesiastes and Jesus used parables and one-liners to goad people into working things out for themselves, so does Nietzsche. Through Zarathustra he speaks of the need to go beyond the traditional 'good and evil' and proceed to what he called 'the transvaluation of all values'. Nietzsche does not give us ethical answers through Zarathustra, but rather challenges us to go out and create them ourselves. But how are we to do that?

First we need to take stock of where we are. We live on this side of the Enlightenment, a cultural divide so important that it has been called the Second Axial Period. Today people in the secular world are freer from cultural restraints than they have ever been. Does this mean that they are becoming immoral? It may at first seem so, for many observers are alarmed by what they see as an increase in immoral activity and antisocial behaviour ranging from petty crime and personal violence to fraudulent activity and gross injustice on the grand scale. But this may be quite understandable at a time when the human race is still 'coming of age'. As with adolescents, not all people are equally ready to handle the increased degree of moral freedom we now enjoy.

On the other hand, perhaps we should take heart from advances we have made. Look, for example, at positive changes that took place during the twentieth century: the growing recognition of human rights, the acknowledgement of gender equality, the condemnation of racism and religious bigotry, the acceptance of sexual diversity and the realisation that ongoing cultural evolution continues to reveal human creativity. Having witnessed an increase in ethical sensitivity at the leading edge of human culture, may we not discern in the post-Enlightenment global world the embryonic emergence of a universal human culture now seeking to be born?

This is expressed nationally in the spread of democracy and internationally in the creation of the United Nations. Admittedly, the twentieth century witnessed the most widespread wars ever fought on the planet, but it has also witnessed an increasing condemnation of war as a means of settling international disputes and a growing determination to promote the kind of international cooperation that will achieve world peace and harmony. That war is no longer glorified can be seen in the fact that what had long been called Ministries of War were in the twentieth century re-labelled Ministries of Defence.

Whence comes this desire for peace and harmony? What motivates us to try and do what is right? In each of the great religious traditions some have asserted that such moral progress must necessarily spring from some divine command or revelation. But that is no longer the case today. Indeed, many of the ethical advances made in recent centuries have been strongly opposed by the traditional religions.

Some assert that we all have a moral guide built in to us—we call it our conscience—and it is that which motivates us to do the right. That is partly true. Indeed, our psyche seems to come already programmed to develop an awareness of right and wrong. But because this innate inclination is powerfully shaped by cultural forces, it is by no means infallible. Conscience may prick us when we are on the verge of an action in conflict with our basic cultural beliefs, but even when it performs at its best—and in some people that seems to occur rather infrequently—it operates within parameters already put in place by the formative culture.

For example, until a century or so ago many people in the Western world experienced a bad conscience if they absented themselves from church without legitimate excuse or performed useful labour on the Sabbath. At the beginning of the twentieth century these feelings were still dominant, as I can personally testify; but by the beginning of the twenty-first century, the importance of Sabbath observance had greatly waned. I think it likely that what replaced it was an emerging condemnation of such things as racism and militarism, which previously did not worry us at all.

An important consequence of the Enlightenment was to distinguish between those duties that relate to a specific culture and the God it worshipped, and those that are recognised as being universal to all humans, irrespective of culture, religion, colour and race. In this regard, it is worth noting that the Decalogue or Ten Commandments made no clear distinction between ritualistic and ethical duties.

These latter demands arise out of the cluster of human values that have surfaced in all advanced cultures—values such as love, justice, truth, compassion and social harmony. These qualities supply the raw material for ethics because they arise from the human condition. The more we see ourselves in one another, the more these values come into play, urging us to act in certain ways. Our psyche is programmed to recognise and respond positively to our own likeness in others. That is why children find themselves drawn to those of their own age. By the same token, of course, we tend to avoid or treat as potentially dangerous those who differ markedly from ourselves.

Our moral duties arose initially out of our relationships with those closest to us—the family, the tribe, the nation. 'Do unto others what you would have them do to you!' That is why, in the evolution of morality, this Golden Rule came to be enunciated in several cultures quite independently. Eventually we began to acknowledge that our common humanity reached across ethnic and cultural barriers, until at the present time it is in the process of becoming global.

But however noble and universal the Golden Rule is, it remains a rule of thumb and is only a start. For the values that motivate us to perform our moral duties may themselves come into conflict. For example, reverence for life clashes with compassion in the clinical abortion debate and in the controversy over euthanasia. In the latter case, for example, it can lead to the seeming inconsistency that it is incumbent upon us to put a mortally wounded animal out of its misery, but wrong to end the lives of humans who suffer in agony from a mortal disease.

Such examples illustrate why we must create a new ethic. We cannot simply pluck out of the air clear and absolute answers to our moral problems; rather we have to work through each of them as best we can.

This is why the *Situation Ethics* of Joseph Fletcher has become so timely. His book was published in 1966, three years after *Honest to God*, and John Robinson referred to it as 'the only ethic for man come of age'. The idea aroused vigorous opposition and condemnation from people who had not understood or come to terms with the new cultural age we have entered. That is why I sketched the cultural history that led up to this age. We have entered an age in which there are values to be honoured and defended, but few if any moral absolutes. In an age where so much is seen to be relative to time and place, the guide lines proposed by situation ethics are very positive. It steers a middle course between the old legalism based on the supposed absolutes and the unprincipled license to do anything, a position known as antinomianism. This is how Fletcher explained the essence of situation ethics:

> The situationist enters into every decision-making situation fully armed with the ethical maxims of his community and its heritage, and he treats them with respect as illuminators of his problems. Just the same he is prepared in any situation to compromise them or set them aside if love seems better served by doing so.

But since Fletcher's book, a whole new area of ethical problems has emerged. Ethics is no longer concerned solely, as it long seemed to be, with the duties we owe to one another as fellow-humans. During the latter part of the twentieth century we have been coming to recognize that we have duties to the earth and to all forms of life on it. Strangely enough, this has placed us in a position not unlike that from which our long cultural story has evolved.

As we noted earlier, until only a few thousand years ago humans believed they had duties to a Sky Father, an Earth Mother, a throng of gods, and all the plants and animals of the ecosystem. Today we are being forced to relearn how much we depend on the natural world. Our need for *pure* air, *clean* water, *healthy* food, *adequate* shelter and the *most desirable* conditions for the continuation of our species has once again become the ultimate, or religious, issue to which we must 'devote' ourselves.

This enables us to realise that there was a downside to the monotheistic culture that evolved between the two Axial Periods. Of course much in it was of value, but it also had the effect of turning our attention away from the earth and even causing us to disparage it as a 'fallen world'. Notice how we use the term 'earthy' to refer to objects and practices we think we should distance ourselves from. In those two-and-a-half thousand years of monotheism our minds were directed away from the earth to the unseen worlds of Heaven and Hell that our own imaginations had created. But now that world has disintegrated, and our eyes are being opened to the realities of this world. We are coming back to earth with a sudden bump, and to our dismay we find we have been treating the earth too carelessly. We have been polluting it. We have been exploiting it. We have been interfering with the delicate ecological balance that evolved over aeons.

In short, as we move into the future we are also recovering something precious from our long lost past and coming to recognize that our relationship with the earth has much in common with that of the ancients. As far back as 1848, the early modern theologian Ludwig Feuerbach made an important point: "That upon which human beings are fully dependent was originally nothing other than Nature. Nature is the first, original object of religion". In this twenty-first century we are painfully relearning that in spite of all of our knowledge and sophistication, the forces of nature still transcend us.

Because we are dependent on nature for our present and continued well-being, and even more for our future, we have duties towards the natural world as well as to one another. The big difference between us and the ancients is that they created the gods to explain natural phenomena, whereas we have developed the scientific method to help us understand the ways of nature, and what we learn from science better enables us to discern the duties we owe to the natural world. Since we can now acknowledge the earth to be the mother and ongoing sustainer of all life, we have even greater reason than formerly to invoke Mother Nature.

One scientist has gone further and reinstated the ancient name of Gaia. What is known as Gaia theory originated in the mind of an extraordinarily creative scientist named James Lovelock. Gaia theory does not propose that the earth *is* a living organism, but rather that life in all of its diversity has so evolved in relation to the physical forces of its earthly environment that the earth's functional operation is rather *like that of* a living organism.

But whether we call it Gaia, Mother Nature, or simply nature, we are dependent on it, and that dependence incurs duties. But those duties will not be revealed to us from out of the blue as a new set of commandments. Rather it is we who will have to enunciate them. For this we need knowledge—and for this we turn largely to science.

But we also need to develop a new attitude toward the world in which we find ourselves. That attitude will necessarily be very like the religious attitudes of the past, responses that are often described in such terms as awe, worship and the sense of the holy. Churchgoing was a regular time on a Sunday when we joined in what was called the public worship—that is the people's worship of God, on whom we thought life to depend.

If we are to live ethically in this new secular age, we will need from time to time to pause, ponder and

- Stand in awe of this star-clad universe
- Marvel at the evolving diversity of life on this planet
- Value everything on which our common life depends
- Appreciate the total cultural legacy we have received from our pioneering forebears
- Devote ourselves in a self-sacrificial way to the responsibility now laid upon us all for the future of our species and of all planetary life

I conclude with the final words of the Book of Ecclesiastes:

Stand in awe of Nature and do what it requires of you,
  for this is the whole duty of humankind.[2]

Footnotes

1. His words are now found in Isaiah 40–55.

2. My translation, as found in *Such is Life! A Close Encounter with Ecclesiastes* (Polebridge Press, 2010).

Christianity
without Christ

Can there be such a thing as 'Christianity without Christ'? Surely not! The very idea seems to be even more of a contradiction in terms than *Christianity without God*—the title of a book I published in 2002. There I was contending that Christianity no longer needs a theistic God—one conceived as a personal supernatural being who created and controls the universe—and of course that is not the only way of understanding the word 'God'. Indeed, strictly speaking it does not even define the God of orthodox Christianity; for by the fourth century its earlier theism had been replaced by trinitarianism. But since the doctrine of the Holy Trinity is so poorly understood, even by many of the clergy, the theistic conception of God is presupposed in nearly all public discourse about God today.

It was within the context of theistic beliefs that the Christ figure came to be imaginatively created by the early Christians on the basis of their memories of Jesus. Therefore, if Christianity can survive without the theistic idea of God, it is quite possible to conceive of a 'Christianity without Christ', and here I shall try to expound just what that would entail.

Anyone who was present in 1983 at the very first series of the lunch-hour lectures, *Jesus Reconsidered*, may recall an unexpected

This lecture was first delivered in April 2010 under the auspices of St Andrew's Trust for the Study of Religion and Society, Wellington, New Zealand, and published by it as Chapter 3 of *Jesus Rediscovered*.

interruption from the audience. As I was describing the effect of modern biblical scholarship on our understanding of Jesus of Nazareth, someone felt so disturbed by what I was saying that he jumped up and cried out, 'You have taken away my Lord!', and then stamped out of the church in protest.

He had a valid point. In six simple words his protest expressed what many church people have felt during the last two hundred years as the full significance of today's biblical scholarship was made known to them. By showing that the Christ figure was the creation of early Christian imagination, modern biblical scholars have taken away the living Lord of traditional Christian devotion.

It is understandable that many experienced this as a great loss. When scholars began to study the Bible with the tools of historical and literary criticism, the strong disapproval they encountered arose precisely because people felt the loss of an infallible Bible very deeply. But biblical scholarship also has a positive side and has brought some rich gains that are often not fully appreciated.

Relative to today's topic, it has brought to light a Jesus we hardly knew—so much so that Marcus Borg could entitle his widely read book *Meeting Jesus Again for the First Time*. Even though we may have uncovered no more than 'the footprints and the voiceprints' of this Jesus, they are nevertheless much more relevant to the modern secular world than is the supernatural Christ long revered by traditional Christianity. It is the examination of those footprints and voiceprints that enables us to explore what 'Christianity without Christ' might be like.

Jesus, it now seems, was primarily a teacher, a sage who bequeathed to his followers principles by which to live, not a body of eternally fixed doctrine that he expected people to believe. Unfortunately, Christianity has long been presented as the latter, with the result that Christians have often referred to themselves as 'believers' and have jealously guarded what they called orthodoxy, a term that means 'the body of correct beliefs'. This tendency has given rise to the modern quip that Christian faith is a matter of believing what you know ain't true.

When we compare Christianity with Judaism and Islam, the two monotheistic faiths with which it is so closely connected, we find an important difference. The term that better describes both of them is not 'orthodoxy' but 'orthopraxy', a word that means correct action—in both morals and ritual. Orthopraxy puts all the emphasis on what one does, while orthodoxy focuses on what one believes.

Why did Christianity come to put such emphasis on right belief? Partly because it evolved within the intellectual climate of ancient Greek culture. During the very fluid period of early Christianity a significant shift from orthopraxy to orthodoxy began to take place. Let me attempt to sketch this shift by outlining the limited evidence that has survived. At the outset, as we shall presently see, Christianity could rightly have been described as Judeo-Christian orthopraxy. Perhaps we could even call it 'Christianity without Christ'.

For the teachings that Jesus bequeathed to us focused not on believing, but on doing. Even before the term 'Christian' came into use, the first Jesus-followers were attempting to practise the kind of life he taught. They called it 'the Way'. And although a few traces of this term have survived in the Book of Acts, during the transition to orthodoxy this term became displaced by the phrase 'the Gospel of Jesus Christ'—something that was to be believed.

What was the Way? An ancient book called 'The Didache' (a Greek word meaning 'teaching') throws considerable light on this. The full title of this book is 'The Lord's Teaching through the Twelve Apostles to the Gentiles'. You may not have heard of this book, for until recently only scholars knew of its existence, and then only because it was often referred to in ancient writings. Clearly, it had been widely used in the early church, but oddly enough was not included in the New Testament, and for that reason it disappeared from view.

As recently as 1873 it was re-discovered in the library of a monastery in Istanbul. And although this particular manuscript can be dated to 1056, the original from which it had been copied is judged by scholars to have been written at some point between 70 and 120 CE. This newly recovered text was soon recognized as one of the most important Christian discoveries of modern times and is now readily available in the collection of writings known as the Apostolic Fathers.

Although the book is definitely Christian—for such words as 'Christ', 'Christian' and 'church' occur at least once—it is not as manifestly Christian as another book from the same period, the Epistle of Barnabas. Despite a number of common elements, Barnabas is more anti-Jewish, even denying any historical link between Judaism and the Christian Gospel.

The Didache, by contrast, is set out in the same format as were contemporary manuals of Jewish practice, and is so close to them that some scholars think its first part may actually have originated as a Jewish guidebook on the moral life before being adapted to the needs of the growing Christian movement. Although it is entitled 'The Lord's Teaching', it is wholly concerned with Christian practice in both morality and ritual; what we would consider theology or doctrine is noticeably absent.

The Didache clearly reflects the period in which early Christianity was still very close to the Jewish context in which it originated. It was written to guide the life of a primitive Christian community around the end of the first century. That is the very time when Jew and Christian were parting company, as we can see reflected in a direction about fasting that today sounds even a little amusing: 'Do not keep the same fast days as the hypocrites'—a term that here refers to the Jews. 'They fast on Mondays and Thursdays; so you should fast on Wednesdays and Fridays'. In a time when Judaism and Christianity were becoming mutually exclusive, it was important for each to establish its own distinct identity. This was why Christians chose the first day of the week as their holy day, calling it the Lord's Day, while Jews continued to observe the seventh day as their Sabbath. (And for much the same reason, of course, Muslims chose Friday as their holy day.)

It is interesting to find that the Didache has preserved the primitive label, 'The Way'. This is how it starts off: "There are two ways, one of life and one of death, but there is a great difference between the two ways". In its short description of the Way of Death we find listed all the commonly acknowledged human crimes and misdemeanours that are condemned in almost every culture. But the emphasis of the Didache is on the Way of Life. Listen to how it continues:

> The way of life is this: First, you shall love God who made you; second, love your neighbour as yourself, and do not do to another what you would not want done to you.

Here at the beginning we find the double commandment of love that the New Testament attributes to Jesus. This is followed by a concise compendium of moral teaching before turning in Part II to a manual of liturgical practice that gives simple directions about the appropriate ritual for Sunday worship, the eucharist, baptism, prayer, fasting and how to treat travelling evangelists. Early in the list is the Lord's Prayer with the instruction that it be said three times a day.

Because of its Judeo-Christian character, the Didache gives us some idea of how Christianity was taking shape and finding its new identity as it began to emerge from its Jewish matrix. Just as Judaism was essentially a form of orthopraxy, so that is how Christianity began—with the emphasis on what to do rather than on what to believe. The Didache is not a creed, but a manual of practice that gives directions on how to walk the Way that leads to Life. It is the Way that had been taught them by Jesus, whom they now referred to simply as their Lord—that is, their Master. Since this is not a divine title but a human one, it is an early expression of 'Christianity without Christ'.

It is not only the Didache that provides evidence of early Christianity as a form of orthopraxy rather than of orthodoxy. The Epistle of James is another document that more closely reflects the teaching of the historical Jesus than does the Pauline theology of Christ. This is why Martin Luther—who based his reforms on Paul's teaching—despised this letter, calling it an 'epistle of straw' and wishing for it to be purged from the Bible. But the earliest Christians considered this letter to have been written by James, the brother of Jesus and leader of the church at Jerusalem. Though the excellent Greek in which it is written makes this improbable, it nevertheless closely reflects the issues known to have been dear to the Christian Jews James represented.

This epistle warns Christians against taking the Pauline view of Christianity to an extreme. Whereas Paul urged his readers to put their faith in Christ as the one who would deliver them, this author calls his readers to action. "Faith without works is dead", he exclaimed. "Be doers of the word and not hearers only. Religion that is pure and undefiled is this: to visit orphans and widows in their affliction and to keep oneself unstained from the world".

In short, what we find in the Epistle of James and in the Didache gives us some idea of what can be meant by 'Christianity without Christ'. It is a way of putting the precepts of Jesus into practice in daily life without having to rely on divine help from the Christ figure. Jesus is honoured as the teacher, not as the saviour. The Jewish character of both the Didache and the Epistle of James illustrates how nascent Christianity originated within the context of the Jewish institution we know as the synagogue.

The first community of Jesus-followers continued all the common Jewish practices, including participation in synagogue worship. What distinguished them from other Jews was their attempt to blend Jewish practice with what Jesus had taught them. They remained in the synagogue for decades, until eventually their Christian identity made them no longer welcome. The destruction of Jerusalem by the Romans in 70 CE led to the scattering of its inhabitants and marked the great dividing line between Jew and Christian, between synagogue and church.

But since the Christian gathering was in essence just as much a synagogue as the Jewish gathering, why did the Christian gathering come to be called a church? Here we confront an issue that has been given all too little attention. We need to go back to the basic meanings of the words 'synagogue' (*synagoge*) and 'church' (*ekklesia*), both derived from Greek words that are virtually synonymous, meaning 'gathering' or 'assembly'.

The origin of the institution of synagogue is not entirely clear, and it may go as far back as the Babylonian Exile; yet it has long had a Greek designation since it was in the Hellenistic period that it flourished and spread. The synagogue was simply a non-priestly 'gathering' of Jews for prayer and the study of the Torah; it enabled Jews to nurture their Jewish identity and give one another mutual support in a non-Jewish social and political environment.

The earliest Jesus-followers not only used to meet within the synagogue but, even as they were becoming separated from the Jewish synagogues, they continued to do what synagogues did— join together for prayer and study of the Scriptures. The Holy Scriptures that the Greek-speaking Christians read and studied was the Greek version of the Old Testament, in which the words *synagoge* and *ekklesia* are used more or less interchangeably to translate the Hebrew words for 'gathering' and 'assembly'. As it became increasingly necessary for Jews and Christians to establish different identities (as the Didache and Barnabas so clearly illustrate), it seemed natural for Christians to adopt the term 'ecclesia', which they already knew from their Scriptures, to distinguish them from the Jews.

The separation of Christian from Jew eventually led to bitter antagonism that gave rise to the anti-Semitism that has poisoned their relations for nearly two millennia. Once again, of course, we know all too little of how this separation took place, for apart from Paul, all the extant evidence comes from after 70 CE and reflects the viewpoint of either one side or the other.

It was within this context that the human Jesus became increasingly transformed into the divine, supernatural figure of Christ. As a result, the Way became replaced by the Gospel of Jesus Christ, and Christian orthodoxy took the place of Jewish orthopraxy. Thereafter, Christianity, divorced from its Jewish matrix, became powerfully shaped by Greek culture until eventually it became what it has long been—a body of orthodox doctrine to be believed.

The evolution of early Christianity has sometimes been described as a process in which the messenger became the message. Perhaps it would be more precise to say that both the messenger *and* his message were transformed into the Christ. By focusing on the way he died (as Christianity has always done) Christians have portrayed Jesus' death as even more than his life, being an extreme example of the love for others that he had been teaching as the Way of Life. Thus, as Paul portrayed Christ and his role, Jesus and the Way were coming to be conceived as one and the same. The Fourth Gospel, as we shall presently see, makes it quite explicit. That is why the original message of Jesus has never been wholly lost, even though it may have been marginalized.

This may help us to understand some of the words attributed to Jesus in the Fourth Gospel. Whereas the humanity of Jesus is still clearly manifest in the Synoptic Gospels, the Johannine Christ is much more than a mere human being. Indeed, as the Gospel itself proclaims, Jesus Christ is the eternal Word—the

Word that 'became flesh and dwelt among us'. What is more, there come out of the mouth of this Jesus such claims as 'I am the light of the world', 'I am the bread of life', 'I am the door', 'I am the resurrection' and '*I am the way*, the truth and the life' (italics mine). Clearly, this Christ figure was a deification not only of the man Jesus, but also of the Way of Life that he taught. According to the Fourth Gospel it was by following this Way that one gained eternal life—that is, life of such an exalted quality that death could not overcome it.

To sum up: what started off as the teaching of Jesus about the Kingdom of God became for his continuing followers 'the Way'; but as they continued to tell their stories about him (even creating new ones), Jesus became the embodiment of all that he taught. He became the Way—the Way to God—to be acknowledged as the Messiah (Christ) whom the Jews had expectantly awaited. Alas, they began to heap such honorifics upon him that they lost sight of the original man and of the radical nature of his teaching, simple though it was. Instead of accepting the responsibility to do what Jesus taught and 'work out their own salvation with fear and trembling' (which even Paul was still acknowledging to be necessary), the church increasingly taught people to look to Jesus Christ as the one who had performed the work of salvation on their behalf. It led Don Cupitt to write, "By deifying Jesus the Church destroyed almost everything he stood for".

So what did Jesus stand for? Why was it that so soon after his death the attempt to follow his teaching came to be known as the Way? Having separated Jesus from the Christ figure into which he was so quickly transformed, we now see his message more clearly. In its 'excavation' process the Jesus Seminar believes it has had some success in isolating the original teaching of Jesus from what early Christians increasingly attributed to the Christ.

At the heart of the teaching of Jesus was undoubtedly the injunction to love one's fellow human beings. That is why Dietrich Bonhoeffer no longer referred to Jesus as the Saviour, but as 'the man for others'. The Didache had the emphasis right when it started off with the double commandment on love. But this also showed how Jewish Jesus was, for while it was his creative insight that linked the two commandments together and made them central, he was simply quoting two passages from the Jewish Scriptures. Jesus had no intention of creating a new religion; rather he was reforming that of his own people. Indeed, Jesus apparently had little if any concern for Gentiles, that is, those people who were not Jews.

Yet what he had to say was so directed to the human condition that it had a universal appeal. It can be said that in fastening on the commandment to love one another he was unknowingly laying the foundations of a new religion. For Jesus went much further in his interpretation of these words than his fellow Jews had been in the habit of doing. As the well-known parable of the Good Samaritan demonstrates, he taught that not only should one treat one's enemy as one's neighbour, but one's enemy might be the very one who shows you how to do it.

That is the why the Didache immediately followed the commandment to love with these words:

Bless those who curse you, and pray for your enemies, and fast for those who persecute you. For what reward is there for loving those who love you? Do not the Gentiles do the same? But love those who hate you, and you shall not have an enemy. If someone strikes your right cheek, turn to him the other also, and you shall be perfect.

Of course we are already familiar with these words, for we know them from the Sermon on the Mount. They show that the exhortation to love, simple though it is, can be demanding and very difficult to put into practice. This is the problem that arises as soon as we take the words of Jesus seriously.

Perhaps this is why the legacy of Jesus so soon became something he did not intend—something we now know as *Christ*-ianity. Though *Christ*-ianity preserved the teaching of Jesus, it increasingly focused on Christ as a source of divine help, thus diminishing the full force of the injunctions of Jesus. By deifying Jesus, by making him into the Christ, the Son of God, Christianity created a heavenly saviour who not only said, 'Come to me, all who labour and are heavy laden, and I will give you rest', but also promised immortal life. Christ became regarded as the source of supernatural power to which one could appeal in one's helplessness.

But Jesus himself did not offer an easy access route to a superhighway that led to a life of fulfilment. He urged people to remake their lives and to make every effort to do so. 'Struggle to get in through the narrow door; I'm telling you, many will try to get in but won't be able'. Moreover, the Way of Life he taught was not just a matter of fulfilling one's ordinary obligations. One had to take the initiative and go beyond the customary duties. 'If someone forces you to go one mile, go with him two'.

Apart from his basic directive to love one another, Jesus did not articulate a catechism or a set of rules like the Ten Commandments. His teaching consisted of little stories, insightful observations and cryptic remarks about daily living. What Jesus chiefly talked about was something he referred to as the reign of God—but he never actually described it in detail. Surely he did not intend 'reign of God' to mean the imposition of an apocalyptic theocracy or the restoration of a political kingdom such as the Jewish zealots were ready to fight to achieve. Rather, he seems to have meant a new way of living together, one based on mutual love among humans, irrespective of race, religion, class, gender or age.

Instead of telling us what the reign of God *is*, he kept telling us what it *is like*. He did this in parables and in enigmatic one-liners, such as, 'It's like a mustard seed', 'It's like a treasure hidden in the field'. He said it means being both crafty like a snake and innocent like a dove. His method of teaching was to prompt his hearers to work out for themselves just what he was getting at. In short, Jesus was a sage; and the role of a sage, as the earlier sage Ecclesiastes so well put it, was to be a goad, prompting his hearers to think for themselves and escape from the mindset in which they were imprisoned.

Jesus used both humour and hyperbole to make his point. People would have howled with laughter when he said, 'If someone takes your cloak, give him your coat as well', for in a time when ordinary people wore only two garments, that would have left a person naked. Similarly, the peasant people would have laughed and the rich would have been angry when he said, 'It's easier for a camel to squeeze through a needle's eye than for a wealthy person to get into God's domain'.

The parables that Jesus told often had unexpected endings. They had the effect of challenging traditional judgments. They were little glimpses of what life would be like if people looked after one another and took full responsibility for their decisions and their actions. The parables were not intended to be entertaining or comforting stories. They were not allegories with hidden meanings, as they have often been interpreted. They were not revelations of the nature of God. Indeed, Jesus rarely if ever made specific mention of God. In speaking about the reign of God he was talking about human relationships in this-world communities.

Take for example the well-known parable of the prodigal son, which preachers have often interpreted as an allegory of God's love for his erring children. I remember pointing out to my fellow theological students nearly seventy years ago that if this were such an allegory, it demonstrated that Jesus had no need to perform any atoning act before sins could be forgiven, for it portrayed a father who, though deeply disappointed by his son's actions, was so overjoyed to see the erring youth return that he welcomed him back immediately without any atoning act or even a pre-condition.

Of course, the parable nowhere indicates it is intended as an allegory about the love of the heavenly Father. It is about a human parent and it provides strong approval for those mothers and fathers (of whom I have known several) who have continued to love their offspring to the end of their days in spite of being bitterly disappointed and even shamed by what their progeny have done. This is a human story about unconditional love, love that does not demand to be repaid, love that continues to be shown even when no apology is forthcoming.

This one parable of Jesus makes a mockery of the various theological attempts to find meaning in the death of Jesus by turning it into a sacrifice to satisfy God's requirements. If humans are capable of giving such unconditional love, how much more should any supposed heavenly Father do so without requiring the atoning death of his son on the cross! It is not only the modern secular world that is causing the disintegration of orthodox Christian doctrine; the authentic words of Jesus are themselves witnesses against its ill-conceived tenets.

The truth is that wherever we find examples today of such unconditional love, whether they are performed by Christian, Jew, Muslim, Buddhist or atheist, there we find what Jesus called the reign of God. That is why Jesus did not come announcing an imminent apocalyptic arrival of a new global order, as John the Baptist had done and as Christianity very soon attributed to him. Jesus consistently yet mysteriously said, 'The reign of God will not come by watching out for it to arrive. You will not be able to say, "Look here it comes!" Rather *the reign of God is already here and you do not see it*' (italics mine).

Those words of Jesus are particularly relevant to us today, when Christian orthodoxy laments its decline in the face of the emergence of the secular world. For the most part, the church has failed to understand how and why the secular world has emerged in modern times. As I have said in *Coming Back to Earth*, the modern secular world not only emerged out of Western Christendom, but is the natural offspring of its Christian matrix. Christian orthodoxy has been slow, even reluctant, to acknowledge the values that motivate the secular world—and this despite the fact that some secular leaders rightly refer to them as 'Christian values'. Jesus would say today, as he said then, 'the reign of God is already here and you do not see it'.

But some will ask how that can be true when we also see so much evil at work—cruelty, personal violence, wars, to say nothing of such widespread ills as corruption and deceit. Let me give some examples that show the presence of what Jesus called the reign of God in today's secular world. We are all familiar with Martin Luther King's dream for America—that all Americans, black and white, would live harmoniously together. In his day it seemed very unlikely that would ever happen. But King was a man strongly influenced by Jesus, and his dream for America reflected Jesus' dream for humankind—the coming of the reign of God. Jesus referred to his dream as the coming of the kingdom of God simply because he was addressing his own Jewish contemporaries, who longed for the restoration of their kingdom and the freedom and political independence that would bring. But his dream was as universal as the God of Judaism was supposed to be, for it envisioned a harmonious and cooperative human community, a dream that was equally applicable to all people. That is why it was able to inspire Martin Luther King.

The success of the civil rights movement in America has largely brought King's dream to fruition in that country. And this is but one example. Think back over the twentieth century and recall some of the radical changes that took place. They may not be as dramatic as the two world wars because they have been unfolding gradually and not without having to overcome great resistance, but they are more widespread and, we have reason to hope, more long-lasting.

The human species is becoming more egalitarian. Slavery is universally condemned and, for the most part, it has been eliminated. Racism, which less than a century ago was so widespread that it was not even seen for what it was, has come under increasing condemnation. We now deplore the kind of nationalism that leads to prejudice and jingoism. Such former class divisions as royalty, aristocracy and commoners have been breaking down and disappearing altogether. Patriarchal structures in family, church, and state no longer exert the authority they once did. Both laws and customs show greater respect for human individuality, and personal privacy receives more protection. Males and females are becoming more equal in status and opportunity. Homosexuals are increasingly free to acknowledge their personal orientation and be themselves. That whole populations have a greater sense of social concern has become evident in the emergence of the welfare state and the recent victory of President Obama in health care reform.

Of course there is still much in the world to deplore—social inequalities, injustice, cruelty, personal violence, wars and waste of the earth's resources. That is why the church, along with all people of goodwill, must accept an important role in promoting the vision of a better world. However much the church has been open to criticism in the past and present, it has never wholly forgotten this role. It is still to be found taking the lead in humanitarian movements, as names like Presbyterian Support and World Vision make clear.

The true mission of the church is not to convert people to Christian belief in Jesus Christ as their Saviour. Indeed, Jesus is said to have rebuked the Pharisees for scouring land and sea to make a single convert. The mission of the church is to keep alive the teaching of Jesus and to demonstrate by its own example how life is to be lived. The mission of the church is to be the leaven of the kingdom of God in society; its role is to exemplify not a coterie of 'believers' but a fellowship of 'doers'.

Jesus did not found a religion that opened the door to 'life after death'. He was concerned with life before death and how to live it. Death is an essential accompaniment of life; it is the price we pay for the precious gift of life. The term 'eternal life' so often found in the Gospels, and particularly in that of John, does not mean life that lasts for ever. It literally means 'the life of this age' and was intended to refer to life of such a quality that death had lost its sting.

Nothing lasts for ever. Astronomers tell us that even the great sun itself will eventually die, but in the meantime the sun exhausts itself by giving itself away in light and energy. That is why Don Cupitt has coined the term 'solar living' for the way of life that Jesus called the coming of the Kingdom of God. In solar living we spend our lives in the service of others, finding our well-being in well-being of others.

The mission of the church is not to proclaim that God has saved us through the sacrifice of his Son, but to help its people live up to Jesus' teaching and to challenge others to do likewise. Try to imagine the reaction of today's capitalist barons to Jesus' injunction, 'If you have money, don't lend it at interest. Rather give it to someone from whom you won't get it back'. Impractical? Perhaps! But just such striking words should goad us into holding the capitalist system up to judgment and looking beyond it to create an economic climate in which the disadvantaged are treated more fairly.

We should not say that the teaching of Jesus is impractical just because it is demanding. It is, after all, the prevailing lack of love and mutual concern that continues to sow the seeds of war and violence. It was the vengeful spirit of the Allies in drawing up the Treaty of Versailles that provided the very conditions that enabled a Hitler to arise. The Second World War was the grievous penalty we paid for not learning how to love our enemies.

Just think how different the world would be today if there had been a different response to the destruction of the Twin

Towers on 9/11. Imagine what the outcome might have been if, instead of invading Afghanistan, the President of the United States had offered to meet with Osama bin Laden at a place of mutually guaranteed security in order to defuse Al Qaeda's hatred of America and together seek a solution that would benefit all peoples.

Just think how the Israeli-Palestinian impasse might be solved if the antagonists took to heart the words 'Love your enemies'. The experience of continued hostility and violence, with possibly even worse to come, is the penalty being paid for failing to do so.

And what of the coming social and ecological crises of which we are being increasingly warned? If the human race is going to survive its ongoing population explosion, global warming and increasing competition for the earth's resources, we must learn how to share and how to care for others. These are the very injunctions by which Jesus outlined his vision of a new kind of world. It will come only if we learn to love one another, including even those we presently regard as our enemies. The future of the earth is in human hands as never before. If the new world does not come to pass, we will have only ourselves to blame. It is instructive to recall that Jesus is said to have remarked, no doubt with a degree of sadness, 'Why do you call me, Master, Master, but do not do what I tell you'.

Contemplating
the Future

CHAPTER 13

Tomorrow's Spirituality

Let me first discuss what I mean by spirituality, one of a family of words derived from 'spirit' that have played such an important role in our cultural past. We have long been familiar with such terms as 'the human spirit', 'the Holy Spirit', 'spiritual', and 'spiritualism'. The English word 'spirituality' has been used for five hundred years to refer both to 'the state or condition of being spiritual' and also to practices intended to nurture this condition. This and all the other derivatives from the word 'spirit' reflect the dualistic world-view that was widespread in the ancient and medieval worlds.

This philosophical perspective divided reality into spiritual essence and physical matter. Trees, rivers and animals belonged to the physical world, while gods, angels and similar unseen beings belonged to the world of spirit. 'God is spirit', as the Bible says. Humans conceived themselves to be unique among all earthly creatures in having a foot in both worlds. It was assumed that although our bodies, like those of the animals, are physical and made of the dust of the earth, our essential selves or souls are spiritual and exist independently of the physical world of space, time and matter. In such a view of reality 'spirituality' had to do with the care and nurture of one's spirit or soul, for, since it was eternal, it would outlast the earthly body it temporarily

---

An address delivered to the Sea of Faith Network (NZ) Conference 1994.

inhabited. Christian spirituality evolved along lines that were thought most likely to promote this goal.

Although in modern times we no longer conceive reality in that simple dualistic fashion, we have inherited and still use a language that reflects it. Maori culture, on the other hand, remains much closer to the earlier world-view than to modern secular culture. That is why such a term as 'Maori spirituality' fits very readily within it, whereas for many in the secular or this-worldly culture of the West the very concept of spirituality has understandably become suspect.

To understand why this is so, we must look to the origins of modern secular culture, which may be said to have originated with Galileo. We are all familiar with the way his exploration of the heavens led to the undermining of the traditional heavenly-earthly dualism. His findings effectively secularized the sacred space that was the traditional dwelling place of God; the supposed heavenly realm was swallowed up by the greatly expanded empirical world of space and time.

In a similar but much more subtle way, seventeenth-century scientists further undermined the reality of the spiritual world when they showed that the air we breathe is a gas, and that gases are just as physical as solids and liquids. In other words they secularized the traditional world of spirit. Spirituality, henceforth, was to become very human, this-worldly, secular—that is, to the degree we continued to speak of it at all.

Let me illustrate this by a little everyday science and the way we use language. In the modern secular world we commonly acknowledge three states of physical matter—solids, liquids and gases. Such a common molecular compound as H_2O is readily observed in any one of these three states: a solid in ice, a liquid in water, a gas in water vapour. As was mentioned in Chapter 8, the ancients, knowing nothing about vaporisation, drew an absolute line between solids and liquids on the one hand and what we call gases on the other. The name they gave to what we call gas was *spiritus* (Latin), *pneuma* (Greek) or *ruach* and *neshama* (Hebrew). In each case the word could mean air, breath or wind. The ancients thought of the wind as the breath of God.

So when the Hebrews offered their account of the world's origin, they said the powerful wind (*ruach*) of God fluttered over the waters. And when they told of the origin of human-kind, they said that God made humans out of the dust of the earth, breathed his gentle breath (*neshama*) into them and they became living persons. Further, it was as obvious to ancients as it is to us that the best way of distinguishing between a living person and a corpse is to look for breath—for a living person breathes. Breath was believed to be the very essence of what constitutes a living human being, and thus the very principle of life. But for the ancients breath, air and wind were all the same. When a man dies, said Ecclesiastes, "the dust returns to the earth and the breath returns to God". When Jesus died on the cross, according to Luke, he said, "Father into your hands I commit my spirit (*pneuma*)" and, "having said this he breathed his last". Of course we are used to hearing the word 'spirit' in one place and 'breath' in the other, but in the Greek original the same word, *pneuma*, is used. Similarly in the King James Version (still nearer to the medieval world-view than we are) Matthew reports that "Jesus cried with a loud voice and gave up the ghost (*pneuma*)".

During the transition to the modern world people continued to speak about spirit without realising that they were no longer talking about something originally conceived to be as tangible as the air we breathe. Christians continued to speak of God as spirit and referred to what they called the power of the Holy Spirit. Preachers continued to expound the story of Jesus and Nicodemus in John's Gospel (where being born again of the spirit is described in terms of the blowing of the wind), but failed to draw attention to the fact that in this story the same word is sometimes translated 'wind' and sometimes 'spirit'.

Only slowly has it dawned upon us that in talking about spirit we are talking about something far less substantial than wind or the air that we breathe. Indeed, spirit has no substance at all. It has become a purely abstract term that has no external referent. It continues in usage as a frozen metaphor from a now obsolete worldview, and its only possible meaning is a metaphorical or symbolic one. Conservative Christians continue to speak about the Holy Spirit, the power of the spirit and so on, as if it were an oozy something that operates like the wind. Without being wholly aware of the fact, they live in the medieval world for religious purposes and return to the modern world for the mundane business of daily living.

On the other hand, to people who have consciously adopted the modern secular worldview and see themselves as psychosomatic organisms, the terminology we have inherited about spirit and spirituality has become increasingly problematic and puzzling. If we continue to use such terms as spirit and spirituality, we must first make clear what we mean by them. Semantic issues have increasingly become a problem with many religious terms, including even the word 'God'.

Where does this leave us? First we must acknowledge that all words derived from 'spirit' are metaphors and are being used poetically rather than scientifically. I nevertheless believe that the members of this large family of words have a vital future in our language because they refer to a dimension of human existence that is not only important but one that we are in danger of losing sight of if we fail to use them properly. In some respects those outside traditional religious circles are making a more effective transition to a viable use of these terms than are those within the fold, simply because the latter are too accustomed to outmoded forms of interpretation.

We may start by observing that the word 'soul' continues to have a useful place in our language even though we no longer regard the human soul as an independent and immortal entity in the way our forebears did. We may say, for example, of a musician, that he is technically skilful but shows no soul in his playing. Similarly the word spirit is useful to refer to a special kind of vitality and/or to the highest qualities of personal existence. We may say of some dramatic production, for example, that it was a very spirited performance. Whenever we feel drawn to make some reference to the human spirit, we are referring to a dimension or aspect of human existence that is over and above emotion, volition and cognition, though it contains and depends upon all three. It is this dimension of human existence that is expressed most powerfully in the arts.

If we explore this dimension a little further we find that it is closely associated with the highest values or qualities we associate with personhood—that is, the state of being a person. This is why such qualities are referred to in the biblical tradition as gifts of the spirit or spiritual qualities. In Galatians 5:22 they are enumerated as love, joy, peace, patience, kindness, goodness, faithfulness, gentleness and self-control.

These qualities, we should note, cannot be labelled intellectual and they cannot even be called moral, though some of them certainly have moral implications. For example, one has a moral obligation to be honest, but does one have a moral obligation to be patient or compassionate? These so-called spiritual qualities are associated with what we regard as the highest manifestation of human behaviour, the highest level of self-conscious human existence to which we can aspire. Thus some of these characteristics denote such inward personal attributes as joy or self-control, while others refer to the nature of our personal relationships with others: kindness, love, faithfulness and gentleness.

Thus far I have been explaining what such terms as spirit and spiritual mean when applied to the human condition. But the word spirituality has a two-fold use. It may refer to what I have described as the spiritual aspects or dimension of the human condition, or it can denote the particular practices in which that spirituality is expressed and nurtured. Of course these two usages have an intrinsic relationship of the kind that should always exist between theory and practice. This can be clearly illustrated by looking at the spirituality of the great religious traditions.

The essence of Islam, for example, is human submission to the omnipotent deity, Allah, the only true God, believed to have revealed his will in the Qur'an. That is the substance of Muslim spirituality in theory. The substance of Muslim spirituality in practice has such elements as these: Five times a day devout Muslims prostrate themselves in both bodily and mental submission to Allah, facing Mecca, the geographical place where the divine revelation took place. Unless circumstances forbid it, Muslims should make at least one pilgrimage to Mecca. And Muslims must study and memorize the words of Qur'an, thus immersing their minds in the knowledge of the revealed will of Allah.

It is quite different with the Buddhist. In theory Buddhist spirituality consists of the acknowledgment of the Buddha's analysis of the human condition: the universality of suffering, the individual's continual cycle of death and rebirth, and the possibility of becoming enlightened and thus gaining release from endless reincarnations. In practice, Buddhist spirituality consists of embracing the Three Jewels—the Buddha, the Dharma, and the Sangha—and of following of the eightfold path to Enlightenment discovered and expounded by the Buddha. This chiefly consists of meditation, the clearing of the mind, the release of the will from desire, and the abandonment of possessions, all of which aid in achieving release from suffering and the wheel of rebirth.

In each of the great traditions the basic form of spirituality expresses and rehearses those elements that give specific identity to the particular spiritual path. Each spirituality claims to be a way, or perhaps the only way, of living life to the full. Each acknowledges, even if unwittingly, that the highest quality of life we humans can experience is made possible by what we have received from others—initially from our parents and family, but ultimately from our cultural womb. We are all products of past human culture.

Thus the key to what we may call the spiritual dimension of our existence lies in what we have received from others, past and present. Our potential to reach the highest levels of self-conscious human existence we owe to the countless generations of our human and pre-human ancestors. We inherit the potential to become human in the genetic code we call our DNA. But this potential would atrophy and come to nothing if it were not for the cultural womb into which we are born and by which we are stimulated to personal growth within the complex network of personal relationships in our immediate family and in society at large.

In his great spiritual classic *I and Thou* Martin Buber contended that to regain an adequate understanding of spirit in the modern world, we must turn to personal relationships. He considered it a mistake for us to think of spirit as some intangible thing within us. "Spirit is not in the I, but between I and You", he said. "Spirit is not like the blood that circulates in you but like the air in which you breathe". Note that Buber was recapturing something like the original meaning of the word 'spirit' but was treating it metaphorically. He was referring to that 'indefinable something' that brings cohesion and quality to the life of a society as 'relation'; it is nurtured by the way we relate to one another at a personal level. Buber chose to call this relationship the I-Thou mode of existence.

In spite of being Jewish, Buber was attracted to the Johannine writings of the New Testament, finding in them much that resonated with his emphasis on the importance of deep personal relations. There we read, for example, "No one has ever seen God; yet if we love one another, God dwells in us and the love of him comes to completion is us". By turning our attention to the essential importance of human relationships, Buber sought to point to the reality of God, insisting that God is not an existing being or object that can be talked about in the way we use I-It language. As Buber saw it, God is pure subject and can only be addressed. We address God whenever we address, and respond to, a fellow human being. Above all, Buber contended, wherever a human community of people is drawn together in a way that manifests the I-Thou mode of existence, there in the centre is the Eternal Thou or the divine presence. One is reminded of the Gospel statement, "Where two or three are gathered in my name, there I am in the midst of them".

In the light of this discussion, what if anything can be said about the shape of 'tomorrow's spirituality'? For many of us, the traditional forms of Christian spirituality that we were ac-customed to are ceasing to be useful today simply because they were shaped to fit a different kind of world from the one we now find ourselves living in. Whereas the traditional spirituality of Christianity was divine, heavenly and otherworldly in character, tomorrow's spirituality must be essentially human, earthly and this-worldly. The spiritual practices of the past no longer fit the spiritual understandings of the present. Theory and practice have become disjointed.

But tomorrow's spirituality will not emerge as an entirely new creation; it must necessarily evolve out of the past and present, for that is the way culture and our humanity have always devel-oped; nothing is ever totally new. Ever since the original creative event that we call the Big Bang, everything we now discern as new has arisen out of, and been made possible by, what preceded. Making the most effective use of yesterday's Christian spirituality will require us to distinguish between what has to be discarded and what can be salvaged and adapted for use tomorrow.

Tomorrow's spirituality will focus on the nurture of the hu-man condition, both individual and social, for we become human only through our relations with other humans. To quote the almost hackneyed words of John Donne, "No man is an island entire of itself; every man is a piece of the Continent, a part of the main". That means that spirituality for today's world cannot be solely or even primarily concerned with self-improvement, introspection or navel-gazing. Such values as are found in personal development arise chiefly as by-products of social interactions. And while we must be primarily concerned with how we relate to one another both locally and globally, we dare not restrict our concern to our contemporaries. For we are not only indebted to those who preceded us, but also bear responsibilities for those yet unborn who will succeed us. It is they whose lives will be most affected by how we relate to the earth and in what condition we leave it to them. In short, tomorrow's spirituality will need to be conceived holistically rather than atomistically. It will take the form of a kind of planetary mysticism, one that acknowledges and takes into account past, present and future. What was once compartmentalized into spirit and matter, holy and secular, will be conceived as an evolving complex whole.

It is because of those who preceded us that none of us ever starts on our growth to full humanity from scratch, having to pioneer an entirely new path. Likewise, in developing forms of spirituality we are not obliged to create out of nothing. And since we can still draw from the past much that is of value, I now propose to look at some of the practices of traditional spirituality, hoping to find some valuable elements yet conceding at the outset that much of their outward form must be discarded because it has been shaped by a now obsolete view of reality.

As we look at traditional Christian spirituality in its great variety of forms stretching from a high liturgical Mass in Catholicism to the hand-clapping and speaking in tongues of a Pentecostal congregation, we may think that none of this is for us, in either its high or low form. But we should be asking what lies behind all these forms and what if anything they still have in common. The fundamental element they share is easily overlooked because it is so simple and so secular.

Every example of Christian spirituality involves a weekly coming together of people to celebrate that which they consider to be of greatest importance in their lives. Let me repeat that: a weekly coming together to celebrate that which they consider to be of greatest importance in their lives. In doing this they are nurturing their relations to one another and becoming a fellowship, a congregation. We in the West are so used to associating this simple coming together with religious practice that we often assume it applies to all religions. That is not so. It applies primarily to Jews, Christians, Muslims, Sikhs and any whose traditions derive from these. Because it neither is nor was a universal spiritual practice, we often miss the significance of the simple words in Acts about the first Christians: "All who had faith *came together* and they *had all things in common* and day by day they *went to the temple together* and they *had meals together* in their homes".

But this coming together did not originate with the Christians; they were simply continuing what had slowly evolved as a Jewish form of spirituality, one that had originated some three to four hundred years earlier. The Jews came to call it the synagogue—a Greek word that simply means 'a coming together'. The institution of the synagogue evolved from beginnings so simple that its origin has left little trace. It was during the Babylonian Exile, when the Jewish people found themselves deprived of their Davidic Kingdom and Jerusalem Temple, that they began to come together on the sabbath day to lament their tragic loss and give one another mutual support. This they did by recalling their cultural past, which their scholars proceeded to encode into the Torah (Five Books of Moses), which in turn became the beginnings of Holy Scripture. The synagogue was not a holy institution like the Temple, for the priests played no role in it.

It was, and has remained, an institution of lay people and it is governed democratically. The synagogue has been referred to as a 'layman's institute', and compared to temples and cathedrals is a very secular institution. One non-Jewish scholar has referred to it as the greatest gift of Judaism to humankind; indeed, the synagogue became the prototype of the Christian church, the Islamic mosque and the Sikh Gurdwara.

When the first Christians came together to celebrate their common faith they were establishing a Christian synagogue. As was explained in Chapter 12, it is largely due to an odd linguistic phenomenon that church congregations did not come to be called synagogues. The first Christians, being Jews, also read and studied their Scriptures, namely the Jewish Scriptures. But by the time we find these writings mentioned in the New Testament, Jews were using the Greek language and the Greek translation of the Hebrew Bible. Two Greek words frequently used to translate the Hebrew words meaning congregation or assembly were *synagoge* and *ekklesia*. By the time the New Testament was written, however, Jews and Christians were becoming mutually exclusive and needed to distinguish themselves from each other; therefore, since the Jews had already laid claim to the word 'synagogue', the Christians adopted the word 'ecclesia' (church) already present in the Greek version of the Jewish Bible. This is the reason why, during the latter part of the first century, Christian churches were still very much like Jewish synagogues; they were fellowships of lay people governed or ministered to not by priests but by overseers, elders and servers. This was acknowledged many centuries later by the Protestant Reformers when they replaced the priesthood with an order of ministry consisting of teaching elders and ruling elders. In the nineteenth century the Plymouth Brethren took it a stage further, setting out to restore primitive Christianity in its pristine purity by abandoning an ordained ministry altogether.

But now let us look at the chief spiritual practice that characterised Christian churches. Even to this day most of the ecclesiastical streams into which Christianity has become divided regard as their central celebration of spirituality what is variously called the Mass, the Eucharist, the Lord's Supper or Holy Communion. If we trace this ritual back to its point of origin, we may be surprised to find what a this-worldly origin it had. The Christian Eucharist did not originate with Jesus and the Last Supper, though that tradition came more and more to shape it as time went on. Behind the Christian Eucharist was the Jewish Kiddush. This is a simple sharing of bread and wine at the end of the meeting together as the synagogue. Once when I attended a sabbath day service in a liberal synagogue, I was surprised to find myself invited to participate in the bread and wine of the Kiddush. There was nothing exclusive about it, as later became the case with the Christian Eucharist. It is a cementing of the bonds of personal relationship of all those present, both to one another and to their spiritual ancestors. And how did the Kiddush arise? It was taken into the synagogue from the family setting, where it had come to represent the regular nurturing of the family relationships that took place within the context of shared meals.

Even this was not the absolute beginning, for it perpetuated a practice that had come to be highly revered among the ancient Semitic people, and that has been preserved almost unchanged among the modern-day Bedouin. The ancient Semites, living as they did in the boundary areas between the uninhabitable desert and the often hostile urban areas of early civilization, came to prize hospitality above all things. Hospitality was the key to survival in an unfriendly world, and one had a duty to provide hospitality not only to the stranger but even to one's enemies. To us it may appear that nothing could be more secular and down to earth than inviting strangers to share one's meals, but for ancient Semites this was regarded as a sacred duty.

In tracing the forms of Christian spirituality back to their roots and stripping away the supernatural trappings that accumulated around them over the centuries, we find ourselves unexpectedly back to something like the present secular context. In coming together to share the doubts, problems and humanly based faith in which we largely share, we are doing something like the Babylonian Jews mourning their loss and the first Christians lamenting the death of their teacher, Jesus. Of course we see and interpret the world and human existence very differently from the way they did, but we stand in a direct line of succession to them and we owe a great deal to our Jewish and Christian spiritual forebears. Moreover, in this simple coming together for mutual support and stimulation we are celebrating our common human and cultural links with them.

It is important not to disown the cultural past that has enabled us to be what we are, but as Nietzsche said, "One repays a teacher badly by remaining only a pupil". We need to exercise a critical acceptance of our cultural heritage. Much of its spirituality will have to be abandoned: its authoritarianism, its exclusivism, its patriarchal character, its otherworldliness, its sexism, its slave mentality and its condemnation of individuality. But we can draw upon and develop its basic concern with our common humanity, its focus on fellowship and hospitality, its goals for a nobler future and the human values that permeate its message.

Just what particular forms tomorrow's spirituality will take are not for me or any other single person to prescribe, but it is incumbent on all of us to assist in their evolution. And since we must create them out of the shared past that I have attempted to delineate, I expect them to reflect these criteria:

- evolving out of the best of the past
- not complex but simple
- not rigid but flexible
- not exclusive but inclusive
- encouraging active participation by all

- transcending class, gender, race, 'religion'
- celebrating our common humanity
- celebrating our mystical relationship with the earth and all its living forms
- leading us to experience awe and wonder as we contemplate this vast universe, the evolution of planetary life in all of its diversity and the privilege we enjoy in being alive

In tomorrow's spirituality (to borrow the words of the Catholic priest Thomas Berry) "We must move beyond a spirituality focused simply on the divine and the human to a spirituality concerned with survival of the natural world in its full splendour, its fertility, and its integral well-being as the larger spiritual community to which we belong."

Spirituality
for an
Ecological Age

Though we still number our years from the birth of Christ, we have come to the end of the Christian Era. In the book *The World to Come*, I suggested that the year 2000 could be taken to mark the end of the last Christian millennium and the beginning of the first millennium of the Global Era. The reason for this is that we are today caught up in a process of cultural change more rapid, more deeply rooted and more widespread than ever before in human history. Although it is largely out of the Christian West that the modern world has emerged, we are suffering the loss of what we long took to be the verities and certainties of Christian spirituality.

We are now entering a post-Christian era. We may call it the Global Era because all nations, races and cultures are being drawn together by trade, the mass media and a common body of knowledge, in such a way that they are becoming increasingly interdependent. Humankind must now learn to live together in unity and peace as one global family. But it also must learn to live in harmony with the natural forces of the planet, or what we often call Nature. This aspect of the demands of the Global Era means that it may also be called the Ecological Age. If the human species fails to live at peace with itself and with the planet, it could result in the ultimate extinction of the human species.

First delivered in 2004 to the Wellington Branch of the New Zealand Forest and Bird Society.

We first contemplated that possibility during the Cold War and the fear of a thermonuclear holocaust.

To achieve harmony with one another and with Planet Earth we need to create a global culture. Such a culture needs to acknowledge the values and identities of all current cultures at the same time as it increasingly supersedes them. Some aspects of this incipient global culture are already appearing in the many new international networks, both economic and cultural. But there is one thing still missing. This is well illustrated by the current distrust between the Western world and the Islamic world.

Every culture in the past has had a religious dimension. This gave unity to the culture, motivating it and providing it with its values and goals. But the word 'religion', in popular usage, has become associated with an outdated supernatural world. If there is to be any profitable discussion about the religious dimension of a future global culture, we need to return to the original meaning of the word. The Latin word *religio* meant devotion or commitment, 'a conscientious concern for what really matters'; the English word 'religion', while often implying a sense of the sacred, originally referred to the human attitude of devotion. To be religious in any culture is to be devoted to whatever is believed to matter most in life. Thus religion can be usefully defined as 'a total mode of the interpreting and living of life'. But because the word religion still conjures up associations with supernatural and other outmoded concepts, many prefer to replace it with the vague word 'spirituality'.

The religious or spiritual dimension of global culture, if it comes at all, will be natural and not supernatural. It will be humanistic, first because it will need to serve all humanity, and secondly because it will be humanly based and will evolve out of the many cultures which have preceded it. In particular it will evolve out of the Christian past simply because the civilisation of the Christian West directly and indirectly caused the modern world to come into being.

There are some voices from the Judeo-Christian past which are especially relevant. Modern ecologists, for example, sometimes sing the praises of the medieval Francis of Assisi. Here was a man who abandoned material riches and the life of sensual pleasure to adopt the simplest and most frugal of lifestyles. In particular, he turned back to the natural world, long neglected by Christianity, and acknowledged his kinship with all living beings. With penetrating spiritual insight, Francis recognized an organic relationship between nature, humanity and the divine so that for him nature itself is sacred.

The order of friars that Francis founded was forbidden, at first, even to own property and had to live by the work of their hands. And the Franciscans produced some remarkable thinkers— Roger Bacon and William of Ockham, both of whom pioneered some of the thinking which led to the modern world. William of Ockham indirectly influenced Martin Luther, who sparked off the Protestant Reformation, and Ludwig Feuerbach, whom I shall mention shortly.

The seventeenth-century Jewish philosopher Baruch Spinoza (1632–1677) so affirmed the relationship between divinity and the natural world that he began to speak of 'God or Nature', as if these were synonyms. Convinced of the unity of all reality, Spinoza effectively eliminated the great gulf previously thought to exist between the Creator and his Creation, between the spiritual and physical. But he was so far ahead of his time that he was completely rejected by both Jew and Christian. Yet his ideas later flourished in the writings of Hegel, Schelling, Schleiermacher and Feuerbach in the nineteenth century and, in the twentieth, in the Jewish philosopher Martin Buber, the priest-scientist Teilhard de Chardin and the creative theologian Paul Tillich.

Ludwig Feuerbach shocked the Western Christian world in 1841 when, in his book *The Essence of Christianity*, he set out to expound Christianity on a completely natural and human basis without any reference to divine revelation or supernatural forces. Feuerbach already sensed the radical cultural change beginning to take place and saw the need for a new religion or spirituality.

Feuerbach further offended the people of his day by suggesting that the ancient nature religions remain superior to Christianity since they were sensuously in touch with the earth and with nature, whereas Christianity had become separated from nature, and had turned God into a supernatural, spiritual being.

Feuerbach was thus one of the first in the West to understand the absolute importance of spirituality even when understood in naturalistic terms and acknowledged as a human creation. Further, he led us back to the primitive 'nature religions' as the base from which spirituality must start once again. Feuerbach, in his later book *The Essence of Religion* (1848), said "that upon which human beings are fully dependent is originally, nothing other than Nature. Nature is the first, original object of religion".

The most pressing concerns of our dependence upon nature are very basic. They are largely the same as those we share with the other animals: the need for air, drink, food, shelter, survival and the regeneration of the species. Built into every species, including the human species, are the instincts to survive and to procreate. These basic needs and animal instincts were the starting-point from which our primitive human ancestors set out slowly, and quite unconsciously, to create human culture, which expressed in myth and ritual their 'conscientious concern for what really matters'.

For the global culture of the ecological age, we too must go back to those basics. The need for pure air, clean water, healthy food, adequate shelter, the regeneration of the species and the overcoming of all threats to human survival has once again become the central issue to which we must 'devote' ourselves. This is a genuinely 'religious' issue. In spite of all of our modern sophistication, scientific knowledge, technological expertise, philosophical wisdom and traditional forms of spirituality, it is from these basic instincts for survival and regeneration that the new spirituality will arise.

An American theologian, Sallie McFague, in her book *Super, Natural Christians* (1997), sets out to reconnect the Christian tradition with the natural world, even speaking of the natural world as the 'body of God'. In such a way, the spirituality of the future will draw not only from the more ideological and intellectualised faiths of the past, such as Christianity and Islam, but from the nature religions which preceded them. Surprisingly, remnants of them still survived long after vigorous efforts were made to eliminate them. Interesting examples of this are to be found in the image of the mythical 'green man' tucked away unobtrusively in so much of medieval church architecture.

Our very earliest forebears stood in such awe of the forces of nature on which they depended that they created concepts, symbols and a language by which to understand them. The concepts they created constituted the raw material not only of their religion but also of their 'science' (or knowledge). The basic realities they conceptualised to explain the natural phenomena they spoke of as gods and spirits.

We now understand the natural world very differently and we have developed a very different set of concepts. Where they talked about spirit, we talk about physical energy. Where they explained the phenomena in terms of gods and spirits, we do so in terms of electrons and quarks, gravity and nuclear forces, DNA and chromosomes, immune systems and amino acids, neurones and synapses. For us these are the basic components of reality, which explain the nature of the world, the phenomenon of life within it, and even how we human organisms think through our brains.

However, scientific knowledge of the natural world does not in itself provide us with answers to the meaning of life. For the ancients, by contrast, the gods they invented to explain the workings of nature also provided some degree of meaning and purpose to the world, whereas our scientific understanding of the natural world leads us to see it as completely lacking any ultimate purpose. It operates according to 'both chance and necessity', as explained by Jacques Monod, French geneticist and Nobel Laureate.

The chief, and perhaps the only, area of the natural world in which we find evidence of purposeful behaviour is in human activity. In some respects the greatest mystery about the natural world is that, within it, there has evolved the human species, creatures who have the capacity not only to think but to ask questions, to look for meaning and to create the worlds of meaning in which they live. The chief mystery of nature is the evolution of humankind itself.

Many of the particular aspects of nature that ancient humans found awesome can be readily explained by us in quite mundane ways, but they have been replaced in our new picture of the universe by other aspects which are just as awe-inspiring. We know extremely little about what takes place in the rest of this universe. We have no idea, and we may never know, whether there is life anywhere else in the universe but here. Life on our planet has apparently evolved over some three billion years. Our human species emerged out of a myriad of evolving living species. It did so only very recently, relative to the story of the Earth, and more by accident than by any design. There is no obvious reason why we have evolved as we have, or even why there should be any life at all on this planet, since none of our planetary neighbours shows any signs of life. The origin and purpose of human existence is itself a mystery.

The modern study of ecology is helping us to understand the awe-inspiring way in which all life on this planet forms a complex, interdependent whole. All living creatures are organisms or living systems, made up of components such as carbon, hydrogen, nitrogen and oxygen, which are themselves lifeless. All living organisms not only constitute an internal living system but, along with their environment, they form a larger living system, which could be called a 'life field', or ecosystem.

The continuing life of each species depends upon the preservation of a delicate balance between the organism and the environment which supports it. Each organism contains self-regulating mechanisms which help to preserve that balance. When one or more of those systems has its balance disturbed and can no longer function (as, say, in diabetes) our health or 'wholeness' suffers. We become ill and, if the balance cannot be restored, we die.

The earth has provided certain basic conditions that must be met by all earthly creatures if they are to survive as a species. Humans have evolved within those parameters. For humans to be healthy they must be able to breathe fresh air, drink clean water, eat adequate food, and live in an environment not too different from that in which they became human. The more the environment changes from that in which a species has evolved, the more the health and behaviour of that species will show maladjustment. Its health will deteriorate and then it will die. A full appreciation of the whole ecosystem has led some to describe the earth itself in terms of an organism. The biosphere is the living skin of the earth in the same way as bark is the living skin of the tree.

In learning more about the ecology of all planetary life, we have been discovering to our horror how much we are now upsetting the delicate balances in the living systems of the ecosphere. Thomas Malthus observed as early as 1798 that human regeneration had always had the capacity to increase the population much faster than the food supply. But previously it was held in check by natural forces, such as disease. So it needed one thousand centuries for the human population to reach 1.65 billion. Yet, due to such a worthy enterprise as medical science, it took only one century for this figure to rise to 5 billion. Within the twentieth century the human population virtually quadrupled. Demographers estimate that within twenty years from now it will be 8.5 billion or even greater. Already a sizable proportion of humankind is either starving or undernourished.

The expanding needs of the human race then leads to the demand for more arable land. So we destroy the rain forests. But in doing so we (unintentionally) lose billions of tonnes of soil each year down rivers, and interfere with the delicate balance of interdependent forces on which the atmosphere and planetary life has hitherto depended.

Intensive development of human technology is leading to the rapid exhaustion of the earth's nonrenewable resources, such as oil, gas and uranium. The increasing demand for power for both manufacturing and transport results in mass pollution of air and water, the two most basic commodities on which human existence depends. We are increasing the amount of carbon dioxide in the air, which has the effect of changing climatic conditions and of producing global warming. We appear to be depleting the ozone layer which protects us from the harmful effects of the sun's radiation.

What has taken millions of years to evolve and stabilize we now have the power to destroy or radically change in a few decades. An appreciation of the nature of global ecology and of what follows if we interfere with it is only beginning to surface in modern human consciousness. The nemesis now appearing on time's horizon is approaching with alarming speed. We have already greatly accelerated the extinction of other living species by destroying their natural habitats but are now endangering the future of our own species.

We are now receiving early warning signals of a living earth which is beginning to feel the pressure of the machinations of the human species it has brought forth. If we are going to hand on the earth to the next generation in as good a condition as that in which we received it, we must urgently listen to what the earth itself is now telling us. It is sadly ironic that our very primitive ancestors were, in their own way, more responsive and more responsible to the voices of nature than we have become in all of our supposed sophistication.

Modern humanity has had no intention of 'wrecking the biosphere': the current damage to the ecosphere is unintentional and occurs mostly out of ignorance. The ecosphere is suffering chiefly through our sudden expansion in numbers and our rapidly growing technology—and the first of these is serving to exacerbate the second. There may also be a religious reason.

Some two and half thousand years ago a great cultural change took place, mainly on the continent of Asia, that is now known as the Axial Period. This term, coined by Karl Jaspers and discussed in previous chapters, is commonly used to refer to the period of creative and radical cultural change out of which came the great religious traditions sometimes known as the world religions. The current phenomenon of cultural change, now on a global scale, may be regarded as a Second Axial Period in the known history of humankind.

During the first Axial Period the nature religions and their veneration of the natural world were gradually swept away and replaced by the great religious traditions. The latter shifted human attention away from this world to an imagined unseen metaphysical world with the result that the physical world of nature was devalued. Worship of the Earth Mother was abolished and the Sky Father now reigned supreme. It survived in Christianity as the worship of 'Our Father in heaven'. The physical earth was desacralized and holiness was thought to be concentrated in a world elsewhere. Only in societies which long remain isolated from the great religions did the old veneration of nature remain, as it did among the pre-European Maori.

What is more, the Christian myth of origins taught not only that we humans were created in the image of God, but that we have been given dominion over all living creatures. This has supplied divine warrant for all of those who set out to exploit for their own purposes all other forms of life, as well as the rich resources of the earth.

It was this element in the Christian tradition that led the historian Arnold Toynbee to write in 1973:

> Some of the major maladies of the present day world—in particular the recklessly extravagant consumption of nature's irreplaceable treasures, and the pollution of those of them that man has not already devoured—can be traced back to a religious cause, and this cause is the rise of monotheism. . . . Monotheism, as enunciated in the book of Genesis, has removed the age-old restraint that was once placed on man's greed by his awe. Man's greedy impulse to exploit nature used to be held in check by his pious worship of nature.

In the spirituality of the coming global society the forces of nature, the process of evolution, the existence of life itself and the ecosphere that sustains it in all its diversity, will all be the objects of respect and veneration. We remain wholly dependent on the earth for life and sustenance. We cannot last more than two minutes without breathing its atmosphere. We cannot last more than a few days without drinking its water. We cannot last more than a few months without eating its fruits.

Some steps towards acknowledging the sacred character of the Earth have already begun. We no longer restrict the concept of 'sanctuary' to the church building or temple but are giving it back to the Earth, in bird sanctuaries, fish sanctuaries and so on. The ecosphere itself is in the process of being resanctified.

The loving care of Mother Earth, and all which that involves, is to a large extent replacing the former sense of obedience to the Heavenly Father.

The word salvation, until very recently, was chiefly concerned with the saving of human souls. It was in that sense that the Salvation Army was founded not much more than a hundred years ago. By the end of last century we had become more used to hearing the word 'save' in conservation issues. 'Save Manapouri', 'Save the whales', 'Save the black robin'.

Life is so precious and the evolutionary universe so mysterious that these should be more than enough to induce in us that sense of awe and joyful gratitude which played such a role in past religious experience. The religious rituals of the future will celebrate the wonder of the universe and the mystery of life. They will revolve around the natural processes which have brought life into being and which continue to sustain it. It is salutary to remember that the great annual Christian festivals (most of which Christianity inherited from Judaism) all originated as festivals celebrating the changing seasons of nature. The Jewish festivals of Passover and Unleavened Bread, which later became the Christian Easter, originated as early spring festivals celebrating the resurrection of nature to new life after the death of winter. The Feast of Pentecost originated as the early harvest festival. The Jewish Feast of Booths originated as the vintage festival. Christmas originated as a New Year festival celebrating the passing of the shortest day and the return of the sun. As humankind recovers full appreciation of how much our earthly life depends upon the conditions and processes of the Earth itself, it will re-create the appropriate nature festivals to celebrate it.

The new religious rituals will be based not only on our relationship to the natural world. They will also celebrate everything we have come to value in human existence, such as the importance of healthy human relationships, and the rich inheritance of human culture. This trend is already observable in the way Christians celebrate their chief ritual, known variously as Holy Communion, the Lord's Supper or the Eucharist. For some time it has been interpreted less as the commemoration of a sacrifice offered on an altar to God and more as the sharing of a common meal round a table to celebrate the rich and sacred character of human fellowship. That indeed is how it actually began.

In a similar fashion Christmas, which is just as popular as ever, is already changing from being a commemoration of the birthday of the supposed Saviour of the world to a celebration of family life. Much to the chagrin of traditional Christian clergy, what still survives as the most widespread celebration of Easter are the Easter eggs and the Easter bunnies which point back to the very ancient spring festival which long preceded the Jewish Passover and the Christian celebration of the death and resurrection of Jesus. Our newly emerging practice of devoting a particular day of the year, whether nationally or internationally, to some special feature of human society that is thought to need extra attention, is already a sign of the coming trend for the creation of new and appropriate rituals.

And how will a future global culture arise? It is unlikely to originate with one charismatic person and then spread to different parts of the world, as Buddhism, Christianity and Islam did. It will need to evolve of its own accord. It will not be built on some external authority, since people live today more by internalised authority. So it will not be achieved simply by implementing a grandiose plan designed by a body such as the United Nations. The vision, goals and values to be found in any global spirituality must possess their own inherent power to win conviction; they must appear to be self-evidently true to all humans irrespective of their cultural past.

The global culture will evolve, if it evolves at all, out of the spread of global consciousness—a consciousness of the human predicament, an appreciation of humanity's dependence on the earth, and a willingness to act jointly in response. These are the very things that may be said to constitute the raw material of the spirituality of the coming global culture.

Whereas the religious traditions from the Axial Period onwards each arose at one point and then radiated outwards, the coming global spirituality (if it comes at all) will probably arise more or less spontaneously out of the common human predicament. It will arise simply because its time has come. Just as the cultural change of the Axial Period occurred more or less simultaneously and independently at several points on the earth's surface, so the new global form of spirituality may well germinate at many different points and then take more visible form as those points form a network. In other words, the coming global religion may evolve out of the diversity of the past, as more and more people become alert to the common threats and dangers ahead. Out of a growing shared experience, human creativity may collectively rise to the occasion.

Not only will some general principles and values be universal, but as we have moved into the Global Era the Christian West has been finding that such values as compassion, goodwill and love, long dominant in Christianity, are by no means as unique as was thought. The best of every culture will find a place in the spirituality of the future. But there will emerge different priorities.

To illustrate this let me conclude by taking the example of the Ten Commandments, common to Jew and Christian. This was a very simple code of spirituality. At the time it originated it was quite an advance on earlier codes of behaviour. It has served Jews and Christian very well as a model and people often call us to return to it. But good as it was in the past, it is no longer so relevant to the age we have entered. Even the word 'Commandment' is now unsuitable, for we are free people who choose our behaviour out of inner conviction.

Here, as a draft outline of the spirituality for the ecological age, I suggest the acknowledgment of

Ten Practical Premises of Ecological Spirituality

1. Stand in awe of this self-evolving universe.
2. Marvel at the living ecosphere of this planet.
3. Value all forms of life.
4. Develop a lifestyle that preserves the balance of the planetary ecosystem.
5. Refrain from activities that endanger the future of any species.
6. Show compassion to all living creatures.
7. Value the human relationships that bind us into social groups.
8. Appreciate the total cultural legacy we have received from our forebears.
9. Set the needs of the global society before those of ourselves, our tribe, society or nation.
10. Accept the burden of responsibility now upon us for the future of our species and for the protection of all planetary life.

Works Cited

Armstrong, Karen. *The Great Transformation*. Atlantic Books, 2006.

_____. *A History of God*. Heinemann, 1993.

Barrow, John D. & Frank J. Tipler. *The Anthropic Cosmological Principle*. Oxford University Press, 1988.

Bernal, J. D. *Science in History*. 3 vols. Penguin Books, 1954.

Bryson, Bill. *A Short History of Nearly Everything*. Black Swan, 2003.

Buber, Martin. *Eclipse of God*. Humanities Press, 1979.

Cox, Harvey (ed.). *The Situation Ethics Debate*. Westminster Press, 1968.

Cupitt, Don. *The New Religion of Life in Everyday Speech*. SCM Press, 1999.

_____. *Taking Leave of God*. SCM Press, 1980.

Davies, Paul. *God and the New Physics*. Penguin Books, 1983.

_____. *The Mind of God*. Penguin Books, 1992.

Dawkins, Richard. *The God Delusion*. Bantam Press, 2006.

Dickie, John. *The Organism of Christian Truth*. James Clarke & Co, 1930.

Feuerbach, Ludwig. *The Essence of Christianity*. Harper Torchbooks, 1957.

_____. *Principles of the Philosophy of the Future*. The Bobbs-Merrill Company, 1966.

_____. *Thoughts on Death and Immortality*. University of California Press, 1980.

Fletcher, Joseph. *Situation Ethics*. SCM Press, 1966.

Geering, Lloyd. *Christian Faith at the Crossroads*. Polebridge Press, 2001 (a revised edition of *Faith's New Age*).

_____. *Christianity without God*. Polebridge Press, 2002.

_____. *Faith's New Age*. Collins, 1980.

_____. *From the Big Bang to God*. Polebridge Press, 2013.

_____. *God in the New World.* Hodder & Stoughton, 1968.

_____. *Is Christianity Going Anywhere?* St Andrew's Trust, 2004.

_____. *Jesus Rediscovered.* St Andrew's Trust, 2010.

_____. *Tomorrow's God.* Polebridge Press, 2000.

_____. *The World to Come.* Polebridge Press, 1999.

_____. *Wrestling with God,* Bridget Williams Books, 2006.

Hartshorne, M. Holmes. *The Faith to Doubt.* Prentice-Hall Inc., 1963.

Hutchison, John A. *Paths of Faith.* McGraw-Hill Book Company, 1981.

Jung, Carl G. *Man and His Symbols.* Dell Publishing Co., 1968.

Kähler, Martin. *The So-called Historical Jesus and the Historic Biblical Christ.* Fortress Press, 1964.

Lake, Kirsopp. *The Religion of Yesterday and Tomorrow.* Boston & New York: Houghton Mifflin Company, 1925.

McFague, Sallie. *Super, Natural Christians.* Fortress Press, 1997.

Macquarrie, John. *In Search of Deity.* SCM Press, 1984.

Matthews, Robert. *Unravelling the Mind of God.* Virgin Book, 1992.

Otto, Rudolf. *The Idea of the Holy.* Oxford University Press, 1923.

Robinson, John A. T. *Honest to God.* SCM Press, 1963.

_____. *The New Reformation?* SCM Press, 1965.

_____ & David L. Edwards. *The Honest to God Debate.* SCM Press, 1963.

Schleiermacher, Friedrich, *The Christian Faith.* T. & T. Clark, 1928.

_____. *On Religion.* Harper Torchbooks, 1958.

Smith, Ronald Gregor. *Secular Christianity.* William Collins & Co, 1966.

Smith, Wilfred Cantwell. *Belief and History.* University Press of Virginia, 1977.

_____. *Faith and Belief.* Princeton University Press, 1979.

Strauss, David Friedrich. *The Life of Jesus Critically Examined.* SCM Press, 1973.

Teilhard de Chardin, Pierre. *Christianity and Evolution.* William Collins & Co, 1971.

_____. *The Phenomenon of Man.* William Collins & Co, 1959.

Tillich, Paul. *The Courage to Be.* William Collins & Co, 1962.

_____. *The Shaking of the Foundations.* Penguin Books, 1949.

_____. *Systematic Theology.* 3 vols. James Nisbet & Co, 1953–64.

van de Pol, W. H. *The End of Conventional Christianity.* Newman Press, 1968.

von Weizsäcker, Carl Friedrich. *The Relevance of Science.* Collins, 1964.

Index of Names, Places, Special Terms

About
the Author

Lloyd Geering (D.D., University of Otago, New Zealand) is Emeritus Professor of Religious Studies at Victoria University of Wellington, New Zealand. A public figure of considerable renown in New Zealand, he is in constant demand as a lecturer and as a commentator on religion and related matters on both television and radio. He is the author of many books including *From the Big Bang to God: Our Awe-Inspiring Journey of Evolution* (2013), *Coming Back to Earth: From Gods, to God, to Gaia* (2009), and *Christianity without God* (2002).

In 2001, he was honored as Principal Companion of the New Zealand Order of Merit. In 2007, he received New Zealand's highest honor, the Order of New Zealand.

CPSIA information can be obtained at www.ICGtesting.com
Printed in the USA
LVOW04s1230120215

426777LV00001B/192/P

9 781598 151565